A Handbook for Adjunct/Part-Time Faculty and Teachers of Adults

Donald Greive, Ed.D.
Patricia Lesko, MFA

Seventh Edition

To order, contact:

The Part-Time Press

P.O. Box 130117

Ann Arbor, MI 48113-0117

734-930-6854

FAX: 734-665-9001

First printing: August, 2011

© 2011 The Part-Time Press

ISBN: 978-0-940017-36-8 (paperback)

Printed in the United States of America

Table of Contents

CHAPTER 6—STUDENT ENAGAGEMENT—WHY IT MATTERS

CHAPTER 7—COMMUNICATING WITH STUDENTS

Table of Figures

Preface to the Seventh Edition

It has been over a eighteen years since Dr. Donald Greive penned *A Handbook for Adjunct/Part-time Faculty and Teachers of Adults*. The book was first written and published with the intention of supporting adjunct faculty in the important role they play in higher education. This book has been purchased by half of all U.S. colleges and universities, and used by hundreds of thousands of adjunct faculty throughout the U.S. and Canada.

In recent years, however, the mission of higher education instruction has shifted. There is a greater emphasis upon student-centered learning, student retention, as well as the utilization of technology in the classroom. The number of institutions offering learning at a distance has increased dramatically, as well. This revision of the *Handbook* recognizes those shifts and provides adjunct and part-time faculty with the tools necessary for successful classroom instruction with particular attention to student success.

The use of faculty off the tenure-track continues to increase, however, and the fundamental challenges remain—almost half of adjunct college faculty maintain full-time jobs outside the institution. They have limited time available for professional development, or extensive reading and research concerning teaching. This publication in conjunction with, perhaps, an institution's faculty orientation program, is designed to accommodate that situation by providing faculty with brief and enlightening information, available at their fingertips for easy reference, presented in a practical informative format.

Patricia Lesko

How To Get the Most Out of This Book...

One aspect of the book that has *not* changed in the new edition is the use of icons to highlight important information for the reader.

Keys to Success: Whenever you see this icon, you'll want to take special note because these are tried and true tips to improve your classroom performance.

Caution Light: Whenever you see this icon, you'll know that other successful adjunct and part-time instructors have discovered what NOT to do while teaching.

In addition to the icons, an index has been compiled for ease of use, and we have added a glossary of online terminology. There are new chapters on student engagement, teaching online, as well as how to teach students about online research. As with the previous editions, the table of contents has remained very detailed to get you to the topic that most interests you at the moment.

> **This is your quick reference for good teaching. You may use this book as a manual, a guide, or for professional reading. It contains practical and informative tips to assist you with your instructional tasks. It is written in a user-friendly manner for your convenience. Enjoy it and GOOD TEACHING.**

CHAPTER 1
TEACHING: WHAT'S IT ALL ABOUT

Orientation to College and Adult Teaching

In the coming decades, teachers of college and adult students will be faced with many challenges. Compared to the classroom of former years, the evolution to the modern classroom has resulted in significant changes. The influx of multicultural, multi-generational and multilingual students, the impact of technology, online learning, and the admission of students with differing academic preparation have demanded the attention of educators. In addition, changing economic and political pressures throughout the world have impacted education and, you, the instructor.

You will feel the impact whether you teach in a continuing education program for business/industry or the military; in a liberal arts college with time-honored traditions and values; in a community college with an open door policy; in a public research university with postgraduate programs; or in a distance education program. Your students will be more highly motivated, more challenging and in many ways more enjoyable to teach.

With the focus on accountability and the realization that there are established strategies and techniques for instruction, there is greater emphasis upon quality instruction. Adult students employed in business and industry expect a planned and organized classroom. It is no longer a question of whether there are going to be instructional objectives and strategies for teaching; it is a question of how skilled instructors are in developing and delivering them.

One of the most important factors, however, remains the human element of teaching. If you enjoy being a teacher, there is nothing wrong with telling the students that you are there because you enjoy teaching. Being cheerful, open, and understanding is always an asset to good teaching. Students will like to hear your experiential anecdotes — share them. Look upon the class as a project. Adult students expect planning and preparation and will not rebel if they are required. Be aware of your cultural and intellectual environment. Strive to be a good and successful instructor and your teaching experiences will be exciting, rewarding, and satisfying.

It might help you to take a few moments before your first class to meditate about your reasons for teaching. This will do two things: it will encourage you to more clearly identify your personal goals and it will increase your confidence.

There may be students who question why someone with your expertise would spend their time teaching a college course. Be prepared. Have a few answers ready if students ask. If they don't ask, you might want to include it in your personal introduction. You certainly have good reasons. It might be to your advantage to communicate them. You may just enjoy teaching, like interaction with others, like the stimulation, enjoy being in front of a group, or feel it improves your own skills.

You should also give thought to your role in your institution. In short "what is an adjunct/part-time instructor?" Too often adjunct faculty, and thus their students, feel their place within the institution is a temporary and unimportant one. Nothing could be farther from the truth. Adjunct faculty in recent years have assumed a greater responsibility to the educational mission of their colleges and universities. Many institutions depend upon adjunct faculty for 50 percent or more of credit hours of instruction taught. Also in many institutions, adjunct and part-time faculty serve on committees and accept other non-instructional assignments. Finally, adjunct faculty often teach in specialized areas where specific qualifications and expertise is needed. Yes, whether you are a continuing adjunct or a last-minute part-time replacement, yours is an important role and necessary to the integrity and success of your institution.

 As with their full-time colleagues, teaching is still a vocation for many adjunct instructors, a calling to those individuals who enjoy being with people and feel an intrinsic satisfaction in helping others to grow.

In your role as an adjunct/part-time instructor, you will realize many of the intrinsic rewards of the profession. You are repaying your profession for its contributions to your own personal and professional development. There is satisfaction in providing service to your community and you will find that teaching builds self esteem, offers personal rewards, and keeps you intellectually alive. Teaching can provide intellectual growth, community recognition and respect, and the development of new professional contacts. The satisfactions and rewards of being a good adjunct instructor are real and many.

Establishing a Teaching Environment

Over the past decades, there has been a major movement in higher education called "the learning college" movement or community-centered learning. Quite simply, this means that learning has become student-centered rather than instructor-centered. This is especially important to adjunct faculty members, most of whom come from the surrounding community and thus are aware of community mores.

When establishing a student-centered learning environment, one should first examine the teacher-student relationship. The simple and most obvious way to develop a relationship with your students is be yourself and be honest, establishing communication in the classroom the same as you would in any other human endeavor. There are, however, additional specific steps that can be taken to establish a proper learning environment. Helen Burnstad describes four areas in which the learning environment should be examined: teacher expectations, teaching behavior, physical space, and strategies for creating an environment for learning (Burnstad, 2000). Although it is impossible to describe these areas completely in this handbook, some of Burnstad's major points are examined below:

- Teacher expectations. It is important first, that each instructor have a clear picture of his or her own style and expectations. The expectations that you as an instructor have of yourself may differ considerably from those of the students in your class. This does not mean that you need to change your style. However, you need to examine the expectations of your students in terms of their position (rather than your position) on issues and principles that may arise in class. Also it is important that you consider your own teaching goals. From this you can frame your philosophy and intent regarding the content of the course.

- Teacher behaviors. It is important that you examine your presence in the classroom. Students will sense whether you really love your subject matter or are teaching the course to reach some unrelated professional goal. A pleasant personality is important. Enthusiasm may be demonstrated through energy and engaging in activities with students. Remember, your feelings concerning the expectations of your students will unwittingly be reflected in the success or failure of your students.

- Physical space. Although in most cases you will have little control over the physical aspects of the classroom environment, there are several things that can be done by the instructor. If possible, you may physically move seats so that dialogue and eye contact are easier. You should monitor the attention span of your students; sense the need for reinforcement; calculate the time-on-task; and encourage students to move, interact and ask questions.

- Environmental Strategies. Some strategies that can improve the classroom environment include:
    1. **Introducing yourself** to your students with some personal anecdotes.
    2. **Being prepared** for students with diverse back-grounds.
    3. **Using an activity for getting to know** your students, whether a game, a writing assignment, or reference card, etc.
    4. **Learning each student's name** and providing ways for students to get to know one another.
    5. **Preparing a complete and lively syllabus**. You can have your students from a previous class leave a legacy by asking them to write a letter for incoming students then sharing it.
    6. **Using classroom assessment** techniques.

Finally, whether one is establishing a classroom environment or doing day-to-day activities, it is important that you be as positive in your student-teacher relationships as toward your subject matter. Make yourself available for student contact, either personally or electronically. Take a personal interest in each student and never judge or stereotype students.

Characteristics of Good Teaching

Using one's mind in the pursuit of knowledge and at the same time sharing it with others is very gratifying. The responsibility for a class and the potential influence on students can be very stimulating. It remains stimulating, however, only so long as the instructor continues to grow and remains dynamic.

The qualities of good teaching are quite simple:

- Know your subject content.
- Know and like your students.
- Understand our culture.
- Possess professional teaching skills and strategies.

Knowing your subject means simply that you have a command of your discipline and the capability of calling upon resources. Knowing students is part of the teaching process and is aided by formal and informal communication within and outside the classroom. Understanding our cultural milieu has become increasingly complex for todays' instructor. Sensitivity to the diverse cultures in your classroom is necessary to succeed in teaching. Finally, it is necessary that you continue to develop and improve strategies and techniques for the delivery of instruction in the classroom.

Some characteristics that students look for in good teachers are:

- Being knowledgeable, organized, and in control.
- Getting students actively involved in their learning.
- Helping students understand the course objectives and goals.
- Being a facilitator, not a director.
- Knowing the latest trends and technology.
- Stimulating discussion utilizing ice breakers.
- Preparing professional materials and handouts.

Setting the Tone

Education professionals and teacher trainers agree that creating positive feelings about the course is an important goal for any instructor. Often instructors assume that students know they intend to be pleasant, cooperative, and helpful. However, this should not be taken for granted. With differing personalities and types of students in the classroom, faculty members must realize that a positive comment or gesture to one student may in fact be negative to another student. Thus, you should make a concerted effort to be friendly. A smile, a pleasant comment, or a laugh with students who are attempting to be funny will pay great dividends.

In setting the tone of the classroom, permissiveness is sometimes a good strategy. We are all familiar with the old classroom where students were essentially "passive" learners. We are also familiar with situations where excessive permissiveness became a distraction to other students. Teachers of adults must realize that flexibility and permissiveness are important to a proper learning environment and that encouraging creativity and unexpected comments is part of the learning and teaching process. The instructor has ultimate authority so excessive distraction can always be controlled. Instructors need not exercise authority for its own sake. Remember, permissiveness and flexibility requires considerable skill to work. Authority comes with the title of instructor.

Teachers as Actors and Actresses

In reality, teachers are on stage; they are actors or actresses whether or not they recognize and admit it. A teacher in front of the classroom carries all of the responsibility for the success of the performance, and this requires all of the talents of anyone on the stage. Due to modern technology, unfortunately, students compare faculty to professionals they have seen in other roles. Thus, adjunct faculty must be alert to the ramifications of poor presentation. Faculty members have within themselves all of the emotions of stage performers but with greater audience interaction. There may occasionally be an emotional reaction in class and you should prepare for it. As an instructor, you will experience fear, joy, and feelings of tentativeness, but also feelings of extreme confidence and satisfaction. Handle fear with good preparation; confidence brought forward with good preparation is the easiest way to lessen fear. Remove anxieties from the classroom by developing communication systems. Some adjunct faculty members are effective at using humor.

As a general rule, however, humor should be used delicately. Jokes are completely out. Almost any joke that is told will offend someone.

Classroom Communication

Many kinds of communication exist in every classroom situation. You must be aware that facial expressions and eye contact with students, as well as student interactions, are all forms of communication. It is your responsibilty to ensure that classroom communication is structured in a positive manner. Communication starts the moment you enter the classroom for the first class session. The communication methods you use during the first class and the initial interaction with students are indicative of the types of communication that will exist throughout the course.

The amount of student participation as the course progresses is an indicator of the direction in which the communication is flowing; more is always better. Since many students today are adults, there is greater opportunity to call upon their experiences. The discussion of facts, events, examples, analogies, and anecdotes will often elicit an association for your adult students. This will encourage students to share experiences and anecdotes of their own.

Do not assume that classroom communication can only be between the instructor and students. Communication in the classroom can take any number of forms. It can mean a room full of small group activities where students are discussing and interacting with each other as the instructor stands silently by. It can also include animated and serious discussions and even disagreements while addressing a specific problem or issue presented in class. As the instructor, one of your major responsibilities is to provide a setting where students can communicate freely and provide an instructor-directed vehicle that maintains positive goal-oriented communication.

. Some specific instructor-led communication activities include the use of open-ended questions, critical thinking techniques, anecdotes, and problem-solving activities. Communication activities between students include buzz groups, a partner system, student panels, collaborative learning activities, student group reports, brainstorming and group discussions. Remember, a good class is dynamic, participative, and interactive.

The Three Rs of Teaching

Everyone remembers the three Rs of learning. For any instructor, however, the three Rs of teaching, are equally important.

The three Rs of good teaching are: repeat, respond, and reinforce. Very simply, student comments and contributions, if worthy of being recognized in class, are worthy of being repeated. A simple repeat, however, is not sufficient. You should elicit an additional response either from the class or the student making the original statement. After the response, you should offer a reinforcement of the statement or add your own conclusions. These three simple rules improve class relationships by emphasizing the importance of student contributions, relationships between students, and the instructor's respect for all the students. This promotes two-way communication and represents the application of one of the basic tenets of learning— reinforcement.

Teaching Styles

Just as students have styles of learning, faculty have their own styles of teaching. Whether your style is one of planned preparation or a natural development, your style is important. For example, an instructor who emphasizes facts in teaching will have difficulty developing meaningful discussions with students who have progressed to the analysis stage of their learning. It is not important that part-time instructors modify their behavior to match that of students. It is important, however, that part-time faculty recognize their own teaching styles and adapt teaching processes, techniques, and strategies to enhance their most effective style. Some questions to assist you in determing your teaching style are:

- Do I tend to be authoritative, directional, semi-directional, or laissez-faire in my classroom leadership?
- Do I solicit communication with and between students easily or with difficulty?
- Am I well-organized and prepared?
- Am I meticulous in my professional appearance or do I have a tendency to put other priorities first and show up in class as is?

 A common mistake for many instructors is that they assume their students will learn in the same manner in which the instructor learned as a student.

Therefore, it would be wise to examine some of the basic learning styles of students, discussed in detail in Chapter 2. By understanding student learning styles, you can modify your teaching techniques to be certain that your presentation style does not turn off certain students.

For example, if you tended to learn best from a direct no-nonsense instructor, then chances are you will lean toward that type of behavior in your own teaching. This would satisfy students who learn in that manner; however, there will be students in your class who are more successful in a more laissez-faire-type environment that gives more freedom of expression. If you thrive on open communication and discussion in your learning process, expecting this from all of your students may be a false hope since many students are silent learners and may be intimidated by the need to verbally participate in class.

These are only a few examples of the types of teaching style adjustments that may be necessary to become an effective facilitator of learning. I have found that teaching styles are not static. Many of the techniques I used early in my career with younger students who appreciated humor and diversion were not as effective later with more mature students who felt they were there to learn, not to be entertained. I also noticed later in my career that although I was well-organized, had well-stated objectives, used good class communication, and observed the characteristics that I deemed important to good teaching, I had become too serious. For that reason I now occasionally mix in with my lesson plan an additional sheet that says to me, "smile, be friendly, smell the roses."

Also, I have found an evolution in the use of anecdotes. Strangely enough it was the reverse. Early in my career the use of anecdotes sometimes drew criticism from students as "too much story telling," or "more war stories." Later I began to put the question on my evaluation questionnaires: "Were the anecdotes and stories meaningful?" The overwhelming response from adult students was "yes." They were pertinent, they brought meaning to the class, and they were valuable because the adults were interested in real life experiences rather than rote lecturing.

 One note of caution, however, the use of anecdotes should relate to the topic being discussed and not simply stories of other experiences.

In general, however, most of today's students will approve of anecdotes and may have their own to contribute.

If you wish to do a quick analysis of your style, it can easily be done using the Internet. One such survey is "Gardner's Multiple Intelligences," available on most major search engines. This survey allows you to examine your strengths in eight categories, allowing you to analyze your own strengths and weaknesses in relation to your students. Although you need to be aware of copyright restrictions, many sites have surveys available with copyright permission granted so you can even use them in class.

A meaningful exercise might be to have your students complete the survey on their own (it is non-threatening) and discuss the composite results and what they mean in class.

Professional Ethics

Although the teaching profession has been slow (compared to other professions) to address ethical issues, developments of the past few decades has encouraged an examination of the ethical status of college faculty. Although the recent attention has been inspired by legal or public relations concerns, there has always existed an unwritten code of ethics for teachers based upon values that have evolved both within the teaching profession and our culture.

Dr. Wilbert McKeachie states, "Ethical standards are intended to guide us in carrying out the responsibilities we have to the different groups with whom we interact" (McKeachie, 1994).

Some institutions have adopted written standards of ethical behavior expected of all college faculty. A compilation of some of these standards is listed below as an example and all adjunct/ part-time faculty should check with their department director or dean for information on their institution's standards. For clarity, the guidelines are presented in two categories: those pertaining to the profession of teaching and those pertaining to students.

Ethics and the Profession. This section is an attempt to emphasize the ethical expectations of the profession and the institution in which part-time faculty are employed.

Adjunct faculty:

- Will attend all assigned classes with adequately prepared materials and content as described in the course description.

- Will not attempt to teach a course for which they are not qualified and knowledgeable.

- Will present all sides on controversial issues.

- Will conduct a fair evaluation of students, applied equally to all.

- Will not promote outside entrepreneurial activities within the class setting.

- When reasonably possible, will attend college orientations and other development activities presented for the improvement of their role as an instructor.

- Will avoid behavior that may be interpreted as discriminatory based upon gender, age, social status or racial background.

- Will hold their colleagues and institution in highest respect in their actions and communication within and outside the institution.

Professional Ethics and Students. This section relates to ethical considerations concerning students.

Adjunct faculty:

- Won't discuss students and their problems outside of the professional structure of the institution.

- Will refer student personal problems to qualified staff.

- Will maintain and honor office hours and appointments with students.

- Will respect students' integrity and avoid social encounters with students which might suggest misuse of power.

- Will not attempt to influence students' philosophy or their positions concerning social and political issues.

- Will not ask students for personal information for research purposes.

These guidelines are quite general; however, they provide a vehicle for examining more closely the expectations of the institution in which you teach. Unfortunately, in today's world, there is sometimes a fine line between ethical issues and legal issues.

More formal statements of professional standards are available from the American Association of University Professors, "Statement on Professional Ethics," adopted in 1987, <http://www.aaup.org/AAUP/pubres/policydocs/contents/statementonprofessionalethics.htm>, as well as the National Education Association. For purposes of brevity, only the NEA's "Commitment to the Student" under the Code of Ethics of the Education Profession is presented here. <http://www.nea.org/home/30442.htm>

The educator strives to help each student realize his or her potential as a worthy and effective member of society. The educator therefore works to stimulate the spirit of inquiry, the acquisition of knowledge and understanding, and the thoughtful formulation of worthy goals.

In fulfillment of the obligation to the student, the educator—

- Shall not unreasonably restrain the student from independent action in the pursuit of learning.
- Shall not unreasonably deny the student's access to varying points of view.
- Shall not deliberately suppress or distort subject matter relevant to the student's progress.
- Shall make reasonable effort to protect the student from conditions harmful to learning or to health and safety.
- Shall not intentionally expose the student to embarrassment or disparagement.
- Shall not on the basis of race, color, creed, sex, national origin, marital status, political or religious beliefs, family, social or cultural background, or sexual orientation, unfairly:
  a. exclude any student from participation in any program.
  b. deny benefits to any student.
  c. grant any advantage to any student.
- Shall not use professional relationships with students for private advantage.
- Shall not disclose information about students obtained in the course of professional service unless disclosure serves a compelling professional purpose or is required by law (NEA, 1975).

Academic Dishonesty

Academic dishonesty usually appears in two forms: outright cheating or plagiarism. The problem of cheating in college classrooms has probably become more common in the last few years due to the pressures on students to succeed. Adding to the problem is the fact that we offer student instruction in conducting research online, which in turn leads to temptation to copy and paste materials found online rather than to conduct original research.

To minimize cheating, some instructors place a significant percentage of the student evaluation in the form of shared or active student participation. These activities are evaluated for all members of the group, thus providing no incentive for individuals to attempt to cheat to better themselves. It is important also that in the classroom environment ethical responsibilities requiring trust and honesty are emphasized. Of course, the traditional method of countering cheating is to develop multiple tests with different questions and to not repeat the same test or test questions term after term.

Regardless of the amount of trust built in a classroom situation, all exams should be proctored and you should never leave the room in which an exam is being conducted. The instructor is ethically responsible for this commitment to the students who are striving honestly to achieve their goals and make their grade and to the institution. Obviously, extra time spent by the instructor to devise an evaluation plan in which written tests are only part of the final grade is time well spent. Lastly, on the final exam, students may be asked to write in their own words the two or three principles that affected them most in the course and what they feel they may gain in the future. This question could represent a significant part of the final grade.

If you suspect or encounter a student in the act of cheating or plagiarism, the student should be made aware of the situation. This should be done in confidence in a face-to-face meeting.

 In the legalistic world we live in, there can only be one conclusive bit of advice: as an instructor, you must be aware of your institution's official procedures and the legal status of your position.

Suspecting someone of cheating or actually seeing is an unpleasant experience; however, it will likely happen in your teaching experience sooner or later. Usually, reasonable rational procedures will adequately cover the situation without the destruction of the student's academic career or standing.

To learn more about academic dishonesty and how to deal with it, refer to the ERIC Digest "Academic Dishonesty and the Community College," published in 2001, **<http://www.ericdigests.org/2001-3/college.htm>**

In addition, you may want to visit the web site of the Center for Academic Integrity at **<http://www.academicintegrity.org>**.

Checklist for Part-Time Faculty

There are many things that you need to know when receiving your teaching assignment. Each teaching situation may call for new information. There are, however, basic items that will almost assuredly be asked sometime during class. This section lists information you may wish to check before entering the first class.

(After reviewing this list, it is recommended that a personal timeline be developed including these and other important dates related to teaching the course.)

Figure 1.1—Faculty Checklist

1. What are the names of the department chairperson, dean, director and other important officials?

2. Have I completed all of my paperwork for official employment? (It's demoralizing when an expected paycheck doesn't arrive.)

3. Is there a pre-term faculty meeting? Date_____
   Time_____

4. Is there a departmental course syllabus, course outline, or statement of goals and objectives available for the course?

5. Are there prepared departmental handouts?

6. Are there prepared departmental tests?

7. Where is and/or how do I get my copy of the text(s) and support materials for teaching the class?

8. Is there a department and/or college attendance or tardiness policy?

9. When are grades due? When do students receive grades?

10. Is there a college or departmental grading policy?

11. Where can I get instructional aid materials and equipment, films, CD/DVDs, software? What is the lead time for ordering?

12. How do I get a college e-mail account set-up?

13. Does the college offer course web site templates?

14. Who are some of the other faculty who have taught the course? Are they open to assisting adjuncts?

15. Where can I find information to develop a list of resources and references pertaining to outside student assignments?

16. Have the course objectives been reviewed to be certain they reflect changes in text materials or technology?

17. Do I have a variety of instructional strategies planned so that my course does not become repetitious?

18. Do I have a current academic calendar that lists the length of term, the end of quarter, semester, or inter-term for special assignment so everyone clearly understands the beginning and termination of the course?

CHAPTER 2
TEACHING ADULT STUDENTS

Although it is impossible to prepare a standard plan that fits all classes, there are some fundamental principles and activities for teaching adult students. Keeping in mind that even these activities must be constantly reassessed to meet changing institutional and cultural needs, this chapter provides a better understanding of today's students so that an appropriate classroom assessment can be made.

Student Characteristics

Today's students, whether they are older adults or just out of high school, possess some common expectations that effect classroom attitudes. These attitudes are based upon students viewing themselves as consumers of a product, rather than seekers of knowledge. As indicated earlier, they will expect well-planned and prepared course goals and objectives. Other recognizable characteristics include:

- Today's students are more self-directed than their earlier counterparts. In other words, they generally know what they want and where they are going.

- Today's students are highly demanding as consumers. They feel that, since they are paying for their education, they are entitled to a product. There have been legal cases in which colleges have been required to provide evidence of delivering advertised services (classes).

- Today's students often come to the classroom with rich life and educational experiences. They have read broadly and often have had interesting employment and/or travel experiences they may wish to share.

- Today's students expect to be treated as adults. They want to be treated as equals, not as students or "kids."

Although the students are more demanding, they are also more interesting, more challenging, and will contribute to a stimulating learning experience if given the opportunity. Most adult students are not in the classroom to compete. They are there to succeed and improve themselves. As a teacher of adults, you should minimize competition and increase cooperation to foster success. Above all, the age-old process of "x" number of A's, "x" number of B's, etc. based upon a bell curve, has been abandoned in the modern classroom.

The Modern Student

The modern student is sometimes described as "the generation Y student" or an "Echo Boomer." Many say that such a label is no more definitive than trying to describe a teenager. Those that dwell on the "generation Y" concept often describe the group as more racially diverse: One in three is not Caucasian. One in four lives in a single-parent household. Three in four have working mothers. While the boomers who are teaching the courses may still be mastering Microsoft Windows 2000, Echo Boomers have been tapping away at computers since nursery school.

In her research paper, "Teaching Gen-Y: Three Initiatives," Dr. Susan Eisner, an Associate Professor of Management at Ramapo State University writes, "To say Gen Y is technologically literate is an understatement" (Eisner, 2004).

Dr. Bob Lay, Dean for Enrollment Management at Boston College, writes that today's students are curious, bright, and highly motivated scholars. "We're getting freshmen who are so prepared for college they're like transfer students."

Accustomed to the Internet, students expect and demand instant service. "It puts pressure on the adults," observes Dean Lay. "We're telling our faculty they better use that laptop and start a web site, because these freshmen want to hit the ground running" (*Company Magazine*, 2000).

According to Dr. Eisner's research, Gen Y-ers tend to naturally challenge what is being said, and have a "prove it to me mentality." In order for you as a part-time instructor to challenge these students, it will be necessary to develop teaching strategies and procedures that will co-opt these learners. These active activities will include group work, role playing, cooperative learning and other techniques described later in Chapter 5. On the positive side, be aware that students today, although expecting a certain amount of autonomy, will respond to classroom activities in which they are involved and they see as meaningful. They will probably be interested in topics and work assignments that can be researched on the Internet rather than in print documents and periodicals from the library. To address their needs for immediate gratification, they will expect answers to their questions in class and comments and notes on their tests and quizzes.

 In planning your classroom strategies for your students, keep in mind that these students want to do something rather than to know something. Class presentation should incorporate a variety of formats including charts, videos, graphics, computer projection and other technology, as well as online/interactive resources.

Teaching With the Techniques of Andragogy

If you are the typical part-time instructor today, you were probably first introduced to teaching using the methods of pedagogy. Pedagogy is based upon the teaching of children and is synonymous with the word "leader" (Knowles, 1990). In the past several years, however, the role of the teacher has changed from being a leader or presenter of learning to being a facilitator of learning because the average age of the college student today is closer to 30 than to the 20 years old of a few years ago. This older and more diverse student body will come to class motivated to learn but with a different set of needs. They are likely goal-oriented problem solvers and bring with them a need to know why they are learning something.

Thus came the acceptance of the andragogical model pioneered by Knowles. The andragogical model is based upon:

- The student's need to know,
- The learner's self concept,
- The role of the learner's experience,
- The readiness to learn,
- An orientation to learning, and
- Motivation.

Andragogy has often been called the art and science of teaching adults because it places the student at the center of the learning process and emphasizes collaborative relationships among students and with the instructor—all techniques that work well with adult students. The andragogical model prescribes problem solving activities based upon the students' needs rather than on the goals of the discipline or the instructor.

Developing an andragogical teaching strategy requires a warm and friendly classroom environment to foster open communication. You must be aware that many adults have anxieties about their learning experience and lack confidence. Thus, plan activities that make students feel confident and secure with opportunities for students to share their experiences. It is important that this classroom environment be cultivated and nurtured in the first class session and that you establish yourself as a partner in learning and not an expert who has all the answers.

To incorporate the techniques of andragogy in your class, it is necessary that you become proficient in executing student-centered activities including: conducting a meaningful discussion, stimulating cooperative learning, developing good questions and critical thinking strategies, and involving all students in the learning process.

Student-Centered Learning

Student-centered learning is more than just implementation of adragogical strategies. As an adjunct faculty member, it would be wise for you to review your institution's mission statement or statement of philosophy. Many institutions in recent years have gravitated toward the concept of student- or client-centered learning. Institutionally, this may simply mean that the institution is striving to deliver their educational products to students anyplace at any time. Although the institution may be striving to meet the individual needs of the students, student-centered learning may or may not mean that the philosophy or purpose of the institution will change to adapt to all of the students' needs.

In the classroom, however, student-centered learning takes on a different meaning. Most contemporary institutions have adopted many educational delivery strategies to accommodate students in many ways in order to assist them in meeting their educational needs. In a learner-centered classroom, faculty are expected to implement strategies that allow students more self-determination in how they reach their goals. This objective is, however, tempered by the need of departments and disciplines to set explicit achievement standards that must be met to fulfill the goals of the academic discipline.

Some questions you may need to ask yourself to assess your goal of a student-centered learning environment are listed below.

- Do I have strategies to encourage **open communication** among students and between students and the teacher?
- Do I have appropriate **feedback mechanisms** in place so that the feelings and the needs of the students are communicated in a meaningful and timely manner?
- Do I have **collaborative learning strategies** in my lesson plans so students can work as teams, groups, or partners?

- Are the **needs of the students** being met along with the objectives of the course?
- Do I **recognize students as individuals** with diverse backgrounds and needs as well as classroom participants?
- Do I **vary my teaching strategies** to accommodate a wide range of students?

Remember, a student-centered environment does not diminish the responsibility of the teacher nor give the students the power to determine course activities. Rather a student-centered environment requires skillful knowledge and use of cooperative and student-involved strategies implemented by the teacher.

Student Learning Styles

One can easily find many paradigms for student learning styles in educational literature. Faculty are not expected to master or study in detail all of these styles and then attempt to categorize their students. It is, however, useful for you to understand some of the different learning styles that may appear in your classroom so that you can give consideration to individual differences. One such learning style system is called the "4mat system." This system identifies four types of learners. They are: imaginative learners, analytic learners, common sense learners, and dynamic learners.

- **Imaginative learners** will expect the faculty member to produce authentic curricula, to present knowledge upon which to build, to involve them in group work, and to provide useful feedback. They care about fellow students and the instructor.
- **Analytic learners** are more interested in theory and what the experts think, they need details and data, and are uncomfortable with subjectiveness. They expect the class to enhance their knowledge and place factual knowledge over creativity.

- **Common sense learners** test theories and look for practical applications; they are problem solvers and are typically skill oriented. They expect to be taught skills and may not be flexible or good in teamwork situations.
- **Dynamic learners** believe in self-discovery. They like change and flexibility, are risk takers, and are at ease with people. They may, however, be pushy and manipulative. They respond to dynamic instructors who are constantly trying new things (McCarthy, 1987).

It is important to understand that all or some of these types of learners may be present in any given class. This makes it necessary for the instructor to possess the ability to use a variety of classroom activities.

I recall an experience while teaching that relates to this topic. Having for years been successful in teaching classes by encouraging open communication and maximizing student involvement, I found myself teaching a class in which an acquaintance was enrolled. This person simply would not respond or take part in discussions. Knowing the student to be social and bright, I was not completely surprised that when all the criteria for grades were considered, the individual easily earned an "A," contrary to my belief that all students must participate to learn! It was only later that I realized that the student process for learning was not flawed, it was just different from the style that I, as the instructor, had perceived necessary for learning.

Closely reviewing the description of the student types will bring out another important factor. That is, just as students have learning styles, teachers have teaching styles. Thus, you should be able to identify your own teaching style from the learning style descriptions. Understanding your teaching style will allow you to modify your behavior to accommodate all learners.

After considering the learning styles above, it is just as important to keep in mind two major factors concerning adult learners. First, they have basically been trained to be cognitive learners so they will first seek to obtain the knowledge and information that they feel is necessary to complete the course work and receive a passing grade. Second, adults learn by doing. They want to take part in learning activities based upon their needs and application. When interacting with individual students in your classroom, you must continually recognize that all learners are not coming from the same set of circumstances.

Diversity in the Classroom

If there is any area of teaching that demands common sense, it is the diversity found in today's classrooms. Classes today are full of students of various age groups, ethnic backgrounds, cultural experiences, and educational abilities. This diversity can contribute to a more interesting classroom when interactive learning allows students to learn about different cultures and differing perspectives first hand through debate and discussion.

For the teacher, however, diversity poses significant challenges. While you must be aware of your students' diverse backgrounds, you must be equally cautious not to overcompensate or appear to give special attention to any one group or individual.

There are some specific teaching strategies that can be implemented and of which you should be aware. When contemplating the course content you should consider the age of the students and their experiences. For example, when older students contribute anecdotes, they usually use their own past experiences. While younger students may prefer topics that effect them immediately. In understanding student attitudes and behaviors, keep in mind that many older students were educated in structured classroom settings and are accustomed to formal lecture and discussion formats, while younger students will probably respond to a more active learning style. Older students also will have the confidence to share their experiences and backgrounds with the class whereas younger students may hesitate.

Above all avoid stereotyping any members of our culture. Salomon (1994) makes specific suggestions concerning diversity in the classroom. Some of his suggestions are:

- Learn to pronounce student names correctly. Avoid the use of nicknames.

- Do not tell or tolerate racist, sexist, ethnic or age-related jokes.

- Do not imply negatives when addressing other ethnic groups or culturally different societies.

- Become aware of your own prejudices.

- Never allow your own personal values to be the sole basis for judgment.

- Constantly evaluate your cultural perceptions to be sure they are not based upon personal insecurities.

Generally keep in mind that the diverse classroom provides several opportunities. Diversity provides an enriching experience when students share with each other and with the instructor and may assist in reducing cultural barriers. The diverse class provides a forum for understanding the differences that exist between individuals and social classes. Through group interactive strategies, these differences can give students the chance to be full participants in their learning and development process. These group strategies can also provide opportunities for all students to become a part of their classroom community regardless of their background.

Bloom's Taxonomy of Educational Objectives

If there is a single paradigm that has stood the test of time in education it is Benjamin Bloom's Taxonomy of Educational Objectives (Bloom et al., 1956). Published more than half a century ago, this taxonomy describes the learning process as three factors or domains. They are the cognitive domain, affective domain, and psychomotor domain.

Essentially, cognitive learning is learning that emphasizes knowledge and information and incorporates analysis of that knowledge. Affective learning centers on values and value systems, receiving stimuli, ideas and to some degree, organization. Psychomotor learning addresses hand/eye coordination, normally referred to as physical coordination.

The importance of these three domains is not so much the overall consideration of the categories as it is the breakdown provided by Bloom. For example, Bloom's cognitive domain is broken into several categories: knowledge, comprehension, application, analysis, synthesis, and evaluation. The affective domain is broken into receiving, responding, valuing, organizing and characterization of value complex. A psychomotor domain essentially is that which provides for the development of physical skills.

The cognitive domain is usually emphasized in the classroom learning situation. However, when writing course objectives it is often expected that all three domains will be represented. This means that you should have objectives in the cognitive domain written not only at the knowledge level but also the evaluation, analysis, and synthesis levels. In the affective domain, you would have objectives covering responding, valuing and value complex. Many institutions require course objectives and activities in all three of the domains of Bloom's Taxonomy. It should be noted from examination of the descriptions rendered here that these domains effectively cover all areas of the learning process.

Motivation

Students are motivated for many reasons: individual improvement, intellectual curiosity, needed employment competencies, career change or advancement, employment requirement, or the completion of degree or certificate requirements. Although these motivational reasons are broad and varied, faculty must possess the skills to motivate students with a variety of activities including occasional risk-taking.

The following anecdote exemplifies such risk taking. After many years of teaching, I remember being faced with a class that would not respond or participate. Admittedly it was a Friday night class; however, you might expect that in such a class, highly motivated students would be enrolled. They were, however, very tired students and many of them were enrolled merely to pick up additional credits. After teaching the class about three weeks and experiencing very little student response, on the spur of the moment during the third evening, I simply stated, "We must start communicating.

I would like each of you at this time to turn to a person near you, introduce yourself and tell them that you are going to help them get through the course, no matter how difficult it is, that you will be there to help them whenever they become confused, and that the two of you (by helping each other) can be successful in this course." This seemingly simple technique worked wonders. The students became acquainted with someone they hadn't previously known, and in many cases, found someone who really could help them get through the course. For the remainder of the course, when it appeared that the class was experiencing difficulty, I simply needed to say "let's take a few minutes and get together with our partner."

When chalkboard work was given, two students would voluntarily go to the board together. Thus a previously unused "risk" activity proved successful—and was my first experience with collaborative learning and the partner system. This is an example of trying a basic technique of motivation. In this case it worked. It may not work every time, but it was not a technique that I had in my repertoire prior to that time. So, when motivating adult students, remember that you must occasionally try techniques not necessarily found in the literature; however, there are proven techniques that should be in the professional portfolio of all teachers, such as Maslow's Hierarchy of Needs.

Maslow's Hierarchy of Needs

It is virtually impossible to incorporate all theories of motivation for your students. It is appropriate, therefore, that we find refuge in a time-honored theory of learning called Maslow's Hierarchy of Needs. Maslow's hierarchy states that the basic needs of human beings fall into five categories:

- **PHYSIOLOGICAL**—*feeling good physically with appropriate food and shelter.*
- **SAFETY**—*the feeling of security in one's environment.*
- **LOVE AND BELONGING OR THE SOCIAL NEED**—*fulfilling the basic family and social role.*
- **ESTEEM**—*the status and respect of a positive self-image.*
- **SELF-ACTUALIZATION**—*growth of the individual.*

Physiological, Safety, Love and Belonging. The fact that Maslow's needs are in hierarchy form is a major problem for teachers of adults. For example, attempting to address the needs of esteem and self-actualization in the classroom, when physiological, safety, and love and belonging needs have not been met, is a difficult task. In fact, the lack of fulfillment of the basic needs may interfere with the learning process. This interference may manifest itself in anti-social behavior.

The challenge becomes, how does one in a short period of time, teaching on a part-time basis to mostly part-time students, overcome these barriers? The fact is that one may not overcome all of these barriers. If instructors attempt to take the time to analyze each of the unmet needs of each of their students, they will have little time to work toward the goals and objectives of the course.

There is, however, an important factor to support the instructor. It is that the need to achieve appears to be a basic need in human beings. The need to succeed, an intrinsic motivator that usually overcomes most of the other distractions to learning, is the factor upon which successful teachers capitalize.

There is little that faculty can do to help students to meet the physiological, safety, and love and belonging needs. The need for esteem and self-actualization, which are essentially achievement, are areas in which teaching strategies can be implemented.

Esteem. Esteem is the status and respect with which human beings are regarded by their peers and activities faculty members incorporate that assist students in achieving status and self-respect will support fulfillment of the esteem need. This is accomplished by providing an environment in which students can experience success in their learning endeavors. Many learning theorists claim that success in itself is the solution to motivation and learning.

One of the great fallacies of teaching is often stated by students who have succeeded in classes where other students have dropped out. That observation is: "That prof. was tough, but he/she was really good." Being tough has no relationship to being good. Often, some faculty believe rigidity is a substitute for good teaching. There is no evidence to suggest that "tough teachers" are better teachers. It is especially discouraging to marginal students who work hard, but find the chances for success negated by the instructor's desire to be tough.

Building esteem through success is accomplished in many ways. The following are some classroom instruction suggestions to assist students in achieving success:

- Make certain that students are aware of course requirements. Students should be provided with course objectives in written form that tell them what they are expected to accomplish.

- Inform students precisely what is expected of them. This means not only the work or the skills necessary for them to complete the course content, but also the time commitment.

- Give students nonverbal encouragement whenever possible. There are many ways this can be accomplished. Eye contact with students can very often elicit a positive response. Gestures are important. A smile, a nod of the head, just looking at students with the feeling that you find the classroom a pleasant environment is in itself effective nonverbal encouragement.

- Give positive reinforcement at every opportunity. Simple techniques such as quizzes for which grades are not taken, quizzes designed so most or all students will succeed, as well as short tests as a supplement to grading are effective positive reinforcement strategies. Comments written on hand-in papers, tests, and projects are effective ways to provide positive feedback. Of course, the ideal form of positive reinforcement is provided through individual conferences and informal conversations with students at chance meetings.

- Provide a structured situation in which the students feel comfortable. The laissez-faire classroom is generally a lazy classroom. Most educators agree that a structured setting with students participating in activities is much better than an unstructured approach.

- Provide opportunity for student discussion of outside experiences. Some students in your class, who may not be particularly adept in the course content, may have significant contributions and accomplishments to share. One of the greatest builders of esteem is to allow students to share their success experiences with others.

Self-Actualization. Self-actualization, the highest of Maslow's hierarchy, is the realization of individual growth. Such growth is realized through achievement and success. Course planning for enhancement of student self-actualization is the ultimate in successful teaching. The suggestions listed here can assist in the student growth process.

- Each class should offer a challenge to each student. Challenges are presented in a variety of ways. If they are insurmountable challenges they become barriers; therefore, it is important that faculty plan activities appropriate for the course. Grades are challenges. However, grades must be achievable or they cause frustration. Achieving class credit is a challenge. Most students, even though they may not achieve the grade desired, will feel satisfied if they obtain the credit for which they are working. Assigning incompletes and allowing additional time for projects are techniques that will assist students in obtaining credit for their work. Questions, if properly phrased, can become challenges.

- Problem solving. The ultimate challenge in the class-room is problem solving. Problem-solving techniques vary greatly depending upon the subject matter. Although it is impossible to discuss in detail the ramifications of problem solving, this challenge does not lend itself solely to scientific and mathematics classes. It can also be utilized in many other courses through discussion, professional journals and literature reports, outside projects, case studies, and group work.

- Treat students as individuals. Individual conferences and development of a system to promote interaction between students, their instructor, and other students are important. Many experienced faculty members do not hesitate to share with students their home or business phone number and/or e-mail address and are usually quite surprised at how seldom any are used.

- Be cautious not to prejudge students. Unfortunately, stereotyping still exists today. Faculty must make every effort not to "type" classes or students as "good" or "bad." Such stereotyping will affect grading and attitudes toward the students. Also, there is a good chance that the judgment may be incorrect. There is no place for stereotypes in education.

- Treat students as adults. Many of today's students hold powerful positions in business and industry. It is difficult for them to regard the teacher as someone superior. To adult students, the instructor is just someone in a different role. Above all, don't refer to them as "kids."

- Give consideration to student's personal problems when possible. Giving adult students personal consideration implies that rules concerning attendance, paper deadlines, tardiness, etc., may be flexible when faced with the realities of the lives of adult students. Practice flexibility whenever possible.

CHAPTER 3
CLASSROOM STRATEGIES
FOR TEACHING ADULTS

Teacher Behaviors

Adjunct faculty can assist student learning with tried and proven strategies. Some principles and strategies to remember are:

- The teacher is a facilitator of learning. Students do not expect teachers to know all there is to know about the subject. They do expect, however, the teacher to facilitate learning the facts and skills of the course.
- Understand your teaching situation. As an adjunct faculty member you may have a variety of assignments at different institutions. When making your class preparations, consider the following questions: Is this class part of a competitive program? Are the goals clarified for the student and the institution? Can student projects be developed to meet the students' needs?
- Allow for individual differences. Every classroom will contain a diverse group of individuals. Allow for this by giving individual help, knowing students' names, and being aware of differing backgrounds.
- Vary teaching activities. Use different activities in the classroom. Try new ideas. Some experts recommend changing activities every 20 minutes.
- Develop a supportive climate. Students should understand that you are there to support them in the learning process not to prove how tough the course is.

- Be sensitive to barriers. Some of the baggage students bring with them include: unsuccessful previous educational experience, time restraints, confusion concerning college (procedures) in general, failure to understand their academic limitations, stress, physical and mental handicaps.
- Be a learning partner. Communicate to the students that you are a partner in their learning. You will develop and work with them on strategy, materials, and projects that will allow them to self direct their learning experience.
- Emphasize experimentation. Emphasize to the students that trying new learning techniques and making mistakes are often as valuable as reaching the right conclusion immediately.
- Use technology to enhance learning. Know about and be able to use the latest learning technologies such as computers and the Internet.

Most of all it is important that you be understanding and considerate. With dynamic changes in the educational field today, you need to keep up with these technological and cultural changes so that they become part of the teaching/learning process. Being alert to these changes will prevent the worst student criticism, "it isn't done that way anymore."

Student Behaviors

During your teaching tenure you will experience differing classroom behavior from students that may challenge your ability to maintain the class in a constructive and positive manner. Keep in mind that the following suggestions are simply observations of other teachers and may not apply to all situations.

- The class expert. This person has all or most of the answers and is more than willing to share them—and will argue if he or she is not right. Suggestion: Make eye contact with a different student in the class and ask for an opinion. Allow other students to react. Give respondent time to tell anecdotes and/or present position, then remind the "expert" and the class that they must get back to the objectives of the course.

- The quiet class. Give positive reinforcement to any response from any student. Change teaching strategies and request an answer to a simple question at the beginning of the next class session. Use questioning techniques, group work, partner system, current events, personal experiences, brainstorming, or icebreakers.

- The talkative class. Direct a question to a group or supportive individual. Quiet class to recognize an individual to make their point or position known. Validate or invalidate point and move to the next topic in the lesson plan. Allow time for conversation, specify time for class work to begin, exert your control.

- The negative student. Initially ignore! Invite the student to a conference, provide success experience, determine an interest of student and cultivate it.

- The off-the-subject student. Allow some freedom for discussion and for the reaction of other students. Other students will usually provide incentive to get back on subject. Seize the opportunity and stress the need to get back to course objectives.

- The unruly student. Remain calm and polite. Above all keep your cool and your temper. Don't disagree. Try to determine the student's position and his or her reason for concern. Listen intently and allow the student an opportunity to verbally withdraw from the situation.

If angry, try to determine the basis of the anger the student is expressing. Ask the individual to meet with you privately during the break and if necessary call an immediate break. As a last resort the class may be dismissed and institutional procedures for such a situation should be implemented. Keep in mind that your primary responsibility is the safety of all students. If procedures are not established, inquire of your institution why they are not.

Classroom Assessment

One of the most recent and dynamic classroom strategies is termed "classroom assessment." Basically, classroom assessment is an ongoing sophisticated feedback mechanism that carries with it specific implications in terms of learning and teaching. It can be used in large or small classes, in any type of class and at any level. Classroom assessment techniques can be used daily or periodically, at the beginning of the course or at the end. The techniques emphasize the principles of active learning as well as student-centered learning.

Specifically, classroom assessment techniques answer the questions: "what are students learning and how effectively am I teaching?"

Classroom assessment techniques are truly developmental, in that no credit should ever be granted for assessment activities. Using classroom assessment is closer to doing classroom research than to developing pedagogical or andragogical techniques. They are intended to provide teachers with a continuous flow of information on student learning and the quality of instruction in the classroom.

The recognized founders of classroom assessment movement, T.A. Angelo and K.P. Cross, discuss in significant detail assessment practices that can be implemented by the teacher. In *Classroom Assessments, A Handbook for College Teachers*, second edition (Angelo and Cross, 1993), they provide a detailed analysis of assessment as well as its philosophical and procedural background. For this brief description of classroom assessment, three of the most popular and common techniques presented by Angelo and Cross are outlined. They are called: the minute paper, the muddiest point, and the one-sentence summary.

45

The minute paper, sometimes known as the one-minute paper or the minute response, is a quick and effective way to collect written feedback from the students. It is simple to use, opens communication with students, and provides an active learning activity. To use the minute paper, the instructor merely stops the class two or three minutes early and asks the students to respond to two questions: (1) what is the most important thing you learned in today's class? and (2) what is the most important thing that remain unanswered or leave questions in your mind? Students write their responses on small sheets of paper or on cards and turn them in to the instructor as they leave the class.

The minute paper question, of course, can be worded in several different ways. If one is asking about the understanding of a problem-solving activity, it can be specified. The minute paper is then used at the introduction of the following class for either opening a discussion of the most noted minute paper responses or presenting the questions and answers that are most relevant. There is no need to ask students to identify themselves on the minute paper since the intent is to assess understanding.

The muddiest point. The muddiest point, unlike the minute paper, asks students to respond to a single question. The muddiest point asks the students to identify what they are not getting from the class or are not understanding. The instructor can specify whether they wish the student to respond to the lecture, a demonstration, or general problem-solving activity. Leaving the muddiest point unsigned and having them dropped in a box as the students leave the class relieves the student of any concerns they might have about their relationship with the instructor and provides an efficient avenue of input to the instructor.

The one-sentence summary. The one-sentence summary requires the students to provide additional information, actually reaching the synthesis level of Bloom's Taxonomy. The one-sentence summary asks students to answer the question "who does what to whom, when, where, how, and why" about the topic and then to analyze those answers in a simple long summary sentence. This technique should be used with important topics and principles, and works well in chronologically organized classes where students need to have some command of elementary principles and processes before moving onto a more advanced topic.

Use of classroom assessment techniques requires the instructor to first determine the goals and objectives of the course, the basic principles the students must learn to succeed in the course, and what types of examples students are required to complete or analyze.

Critical Thinking

Critical thinking can best be stimulated by raising questions and by offering challenges about a specific issue or statement. Many students still like the "right" answer from the instructor but critical thinking in instruction goes far beyond that. Critical thinking involves asking the right kinds of questions and goes so far as to let students develop assumptions and analyze (either in groups or individually) those assumptions. They can then examine alternatives to their assumptions.

Some types of questions to ask might be: "What is the source of your information and how reliable is it?" "What are your personal experiences in relation to the information?" "What arc the different positions?" "What are your feelings on the topic?" "Why?" "Do you agree?" Allow students time to think and wait for some response. If students take a position on an issue, ask them for an alternate position.

Feedback

As has been indicated in other parts of this publication, obtaining student feedback is instrumental to good instruction. Most instructors rely upon student questions and responses in class for their feedback. Good feedback, however, is too important to leave to chance.

The faculty evaluation form that follows and the section on Quality Control Circles in Chapter 5 are examples of feedback. The institution in which you teach may have prepared instruments that can be of value. All such documents have weaknesses as well as strengths, whether they be open-ended or close-ended questions, rating forms or checklists. Given the time constraints facing most adjunct faculty, there are a few techniques that provide immediate and helpful feedback. They are:

- Prior to testing, give the class sample test questions which are not counted toward the grade, and ask them to write responses to the questions as well as the content.

- Maintain open and ongoing verbal communication, especially concerning clarity of assignments and deadlines.

- At the end of the course, have the students write a letter to "Aunt Millie" describing the course to her, then collect it.

- Do not confuse feedback with evaluation. Feedback is an opportunity for you to relate to your students and to enhance your class.

Some additional methods for obtaining feedback:

class discussion
study guides
group discussions
course post-mortem
student conferences
paper comments
quizzes
quality control circles

Faculty Self-Evaluation

Many colleges today have forms available for faculty who wish to conduct self-evaluations in addition to the official course evaluations for the institution or academic department. Whether voluntary or mandatory, keep in mind that most of these evaluation forms in fact capture student opinion and are not statistically valid. This does not, however, decrease the value of seeking student input to improve teaching. Whether you are an experienced faculty member or new to the profession, you will invariably find surprises while conducting such evaluations.

New faculty members will be astonished at the quality of some observations students make. I recall an acquaintance whose associates thought he had an effective sense of humor. However, after conducting a classroom evaluation, he was surprised to find that the students not only rated him low, but many felt he did not possess a sense of humor.

Whether or not the results of student samplings of this type precipitate a change in faculty behavior is not always important. It is important, however, that faculty know how they are being perceived by the students.

There are two identifiable characteristics that are consistently valued by the students in relation to faculty behavior: a) demonstrating business-like behavior in the classroom, and b) being understanding and friendly.

Below is a form that you may use to conduct self-evaluation. Note that the form exists in two sections: classroom factors and personal factors.

The first section of the form (classroom factors) collects student insights into classroom behavior. The final section (personal factors) gives you an opportunity to select personal characteristics that you may wish to review and on which students may want to comment. Questions may be added or deleted to this form at will.

Remember that student perceptions are very often motivated by personal biases, rather than objective evaluation of the instructor; however, continued use of such a form helps to determine if there are characteristics that continue to surface that need attention. Many statistical techniques can be applied to evaluation forms such as this. A simple method of utilizing this form is to ask the students to assign numbers 1-5 to each of the categories and then weigh them on a number scale. It is not intended that this self-evaluation form have content validity; however, it will give faculty members insight into their teaching.

Figure 3.1—Faculty Evaluation Form

Class_____ Date_____

Instructions: Grade each factor on a scale of 1-5 your perception of the teacher's behavior or characteristics. (low=1; high=5, NA for not applicable).

Classroom Factors

Preparation for class _____

Communication of expectations to students _____

Command of subject matter _____

Course objectives clearly defined _____

Course content clearly reflects catalog description _____

Instructor encouraged student involvement _____

Instructor was professional and business-like _____

Instructor well prepared and organized _____

Tests reflected classroom presentation and objectives _____

Instructor utilized student-centered techniques _____

Instructor willing to give individual help _____

Instructor utilized technology and instructional aids _____

Instructor's Personal Factors

Considerate of differing opinions _____

Considerate of students with differing backgrounds _____

Personal appearance _____

Friendly and helpful to individual students _____

Overall rating _____

Greatest strengths_____
_____

Greatest weaknesses_____
_____

Suggestions to improve course_____
_____

(This form may be reproduced in its entirety if desired.)

CHAPTER 4
PREPARING FOR THE FIRST CLASS

Planning Your Teaching — In a Hurry!

Ideally, the planning for teaching a course should start well before the first class of the semester but for many of you this will not be possible since you will receive your teaching assignments a day or two before the start of the semester, or maybe after the start of the semester when the designated instructor fails to arrive for their assignment! So what can you do when you are given a last minute teaching assignment? Hopefully the department has a course syllabus for you from previous semesters, the textbook has already been selected and is available to students in the institution's bookstore; if not, you really are behind the eight ball. Under such circumstances how on earth are you going to give a good first class when everything seems stacked against you? After all first impressions are the ones that count.

First of all you will need to have a course syllabus, or an outline, ready to give to your students in that first class. At a minimum it should include the course number and title, the name of the textbook, (and hopefully the chapters to be covered), the assessment methods for the course (tests, examinations, assignments etc.), and finally information about yourself (name, office number, telephone number(s), e-mail address, office hours etc.) If you don't have enough time to produce printed copies for each student at least write the information on the board, or on a PowerPoint slide, or the equivalent.

Once this routine administrative-type information has been covered, you may then want to introduce yourself to the class – where you are from, where and what you yourself studied at college/university, and maybe even your research topics for master's and/or doctoral degrees. If you feel comfortable enough doing so, talk about your work experience, your reasons for teaching, and anything else that you think might be of interest to the students and which gives them some insight about you as a teacher and a person.

Depending on the size of the class you may wish to employ an icebreaker activity for students to get to know each other. As an example, students could get into pairs (or threes or fours) and each could introduce themselves, their background, interests, intended degree program, and the reason why they are taking this particular course. At the end of the exercise, each student is then asked to "introduce" their partner to the rest of the class. Obviously this only works with small classes. In larger classes you might just wish to ask students to introduce themselves to their neighbors on both sides.

Another possible short exercise is to ask each student, anonymously or otherwise, to write down on a piece of paper, file card, or the like, something about themselves, such as the degree they are hoping to complete, their previous background in the subject (none, high school etc.), the reason they are doing that particular course, the other subject(s) they are taking that semester, and any other interests they would like to add (sports, hobbies, other interests, possible careers etc.). These should be anonymous for you to read later on to get an idea of the class, which can help in the way you teach that particular class.

I always think that it is a good idea to do some teaching in the first class meeting so that students learn something about the subject you will be teaching them and to find out about the way you teach and conduct classes – do the student feel that they are going to be comfortable with your teaching style, and that you are knowledgeable about your subject? Even a short 10 or 15 minutes teaching segment is better than ending that first class early and not having done any teaching. It reminds me of a neighbor who was enrolled at university the first time and when classes actually started was keen to learn about a new subject he had opted to take. He was looking forward to finding something about this new subject but the instructor spent the whole of the first class talking about the administrative aspects of the course but never talked about the subject or gave a lecture. My neighbor came out of that class really disappointed that he had not learned anything about the subject he was so looking forward to studying. It is worthwhile remembering that while there will be students whose only interest is getting out of the classroom as quickly as possible there are those there who actually come excited to learn.

Another option, if you haven't had a chance to prepare even a short lecture, is to ask the students about their prior knowledge of the material you will be covering in the second class. This would serve as an opportunity for students to recall information from a previous course and, if nothing else, helps students to get back into a study mode after their vacations, and to recall information they should have learned in previous classes or in high school. If students are not prepared to answer your questions publicly, you could even try this exercise as an individual or, even better, as a group test. At the end of the test you can ask how many scored at least 50 percent, 75 percent and even 100 percent. At least this way you will know how much background or pre-requisite information you will need to provide in the second class.

The Ideal Way of Planning a Course

Hopefully you will have more than an hour's or a day's warning of the course you are going to teach. If this is indeed the case you will have a little more time to prepare yourself for that first class. Teaching doesn't start with your first class of the semester since a good teacher plans well in advance of the start of any semester.

Among these preparations should be the following:

- Course outline preparation

- Text book choice

- Writing behavioral objectives

- Laboratory manual (if a lab course)

- Evaluation methods

- Assignments

- Developing course web site

- Lecture preparations

- Statement about plagiarism

- Office hours

- Placing books on reserve in library

- Developing pre-tests (if required)

- Preparing procedures on test re-marking etc.

- Developing the assignment attachment

Clearly then there is a fair amount of work to do well before you actually teach your first class. If you are teaching part-time, and especially in large multi-section courses a number of the items listed above, will have been done for you. In all probability the textbook for the course has already been selected, but you will need to read it since this will be your students' main source of information outside of formal classes and so you should be familiar with it. Nowadays most college textbooks come with a whole variety of accompanying materials including audiovisual material, CD's or DVD's, web site information, and on-line self tests, as well as test data banks that you can use to generate test items, mostly multiple choice. Others may also come with student guides and electronic clickers (See "Student Response Systems," page 108). You may also be provided with a course outline, including the evaluation methods, and in multi-section courses the tests may be prepared by more senior faculty with your own responsibility being to just mark the exams. In large classes you may be assigned one or more teaching assistants to assist you with marking. Evaluation, assignments and teaching large classes are all dealt with in subsequent chapters. If a course outline is provided you will need to add in your own personal information (name, title, office number, telephone, e-mail etc.) before it is ready to be distributed to students.

The Course Syllabus

When Erikson and Strommer (1991) asked students at the end of their freshman year about what instructors might have done to help them, one of the three most frequent responses was to "provide a better syllabus." These authors say that a good syllabus will let students know "where the course will take them, how they are going to get there, and who is responsible for what along the way." Lewis (1994) says that a good syllabus will probably be more than two pages long and will contain the following:

Names, number and required texts, (i.e., course title and number, classroom and time slot, instructor's name, office, phone number, office hours, e-mail address, text titles and how they are to be used, etc.) It will also include:

- Introduction to the subject matter and course goals

- Description of evaluation procedures

- Overview of class activities and assignments

- Course outline (including week-by-week schedule of topics, readings, assignments; exact dates of exams, assignment deadlines etc.)

- Course policies (including policies for attendance, make-up work, late assignments; statements about student conduct in large classes.)

Lewis's suggestions for the syllabus seem to me to be excellent and should serve as a good guide for a syllabus. Since Lewis's suggestions were published before the general acceptance and use of e-mail and other computer-based technologies I would also add to her list the e-mail address of the instructor, class web site, blog address (if used), and other social network technologies used with the course. I would also add a plagiarism policy to the list of course policies.

Course Objectives

In previous years it was more common to provide behavioral or performance objectives to students giving a list of the desired outcomes they were expected to exhibit by the end of the course. Even though it takes time to write up good behavioral objectives, they are useful in a variety of ways. Not only do the students know exactly what is expected of them, but it is then easier to construct tests and exams, since the questions are phrased to see if students have achieved these objectives. Behavioral objectives are also useful in deciding how and what to teach as the course material should cover these objectives. Sometimes you may find that the objectives, as written, are impossible to teach, and students to learn, and/or to test, in which case it may be necessary to revise the objectives. You can also start each class by telling students which objectives you are dealing with that day.

E-mail, Web Sites, etc.

Nowadays with the popularity of on-line computer tools such as Desire2Learn (D2L) a lot of the material that formerly had to be typed, photocopied and distributed to students can be placed on a class web site, together with online notes, links to web sites, text references, and even example tests. Such programs can also be used as forums for students to discuss topics from class, ethical questions arising from material and the like. It saves a lot of time if, in advance, you tell students when to use e-mail to send you a message (items relating to personal matters) and when to use web discussion (asking general questions which other students, in addition to yourself, may be able to answer; discussion topics; and as a means of you making announcements to the whole class about test times etc). Discourage students from asking content-based questions by e-mail as answers posted on a class web site are there for all students to read, and not just the student asking the question. Conversely, messages of a personal nature should not be posted on the class web site.

Policies

You may also find it useful to prepare in advance some time-saving procedures, particularly for remarking tests. Develop a hand-out which explains your procedure for remarking tests. A copy of my sheet appears below. You can adapt it to your own needs.

Figure 4.1—Sample Grade Review Policy

LITERATURE 340

GRADE REVIEW POLICY

If you are of the opinion that your paper has been incorrectly marked, you may appeal the marking by following the underlying procedures.

1. If the problem is a mathematical error in adding up marks, indicate this problem at the top of the front page and hand in your paper to have the mark adjusted.

2. If the problem is a disagreement with the mark(s) assigned to one or more answers, document on a separate sheet of paper why you think that your answer(s) is worth more marks by reference to the marking scheme. You should refer to class notes, textbook etc. as and when appropriate.

While every effort is taken to ensure that all assignments are graded in the same way, there will inevitably be some discrepancies. Papers that are to be re-graded should be handed in no later than two weeks after the papers are returned. *Papers will not be re-graded after that date.*

 Another test-related issue is that of students missing tests for a variety of reasons (medical, attending other "official" events, taking part in sporting events etc.) so develop a policy statement explaining your procedures for dealing with these absences, as well. (Read more about evaluation in Chapter 5.)

It is essential to have a policy related to plagiarism. While many institutions have official statements on what plagiarism includes, and how instances of plagiarism are dealt with, it is useful to explain plagiarism to students and how it is dealt with in your institution. If the institution does not have a policy yet, it would be important to have a policy or statement prepared in advance. There are a number of different software companies marketing plagiarism-detecting programs (i.e. Turnitin.com) and some colleges and universities use such software programs to check student assignments.

Figure 4.2—Sample Course Syllabus

Achievement University
Syllabus
Name of Course: English 101-33241
Instructor: Dr. Dennis
Office: B151
Phone: 987-5037 (Office)
dgabrie@ ibm5060.ccc.edu
fax 987-5050
Office Hours: M-F 9:00 to 10:00
M,W, F: 12:00 to 2:00 (by appointment)
Lecture hours: 3
Lab hours: 0

Class requirements:
All papers must be typed. Papers may be revised for a higher grade. Use the MLA format for all papers. Plan to spend three to four hours each week writing.

Course description (per catalog): Study and practice in the principles of good writing.

Performance objectives:
1. The student will organize and clarify the principles of basic written communication.
2. The student will complete critical readings as a basis for completion of his/her writing.
3. The student will develop and increase skills in expository and argumentative writing.

Essay patterns:
  Narrative
  Expository (analysis, contrast, cause-effect)
  Argument

Schedule:
January
10   Introduction to the course
  Diagnostic essay
  Homework: read chs. 1, 2. (handbook)
17   Discuss essay patterns, Ch. 2
  Return diagnostic essay w/ comments
  Discuss essay 1: narrative
  Hmwk: read Ch. 3
24   Discuss subordination, Ch. 3
  Discuss variety and details, Ch. 3
  assign essay 2
  Essay 1 due

31 Discuss writing the introduction, conclusion Ch. 4
Crash Course in Phonics: Punctuation (handout)
Discuss essay 2
Hmwk: Ch. 5

February

7   Subject and verb agreement
Usage problems
Essay 2 due
Hmwk: Ch. 6

14 Support paragraphs
Developing topics
Assign essay 3
Hmwk: Ch. 7

21 Using the exact word
Punctuation problems
Essay 3 due

28 Pronoun and antecedent
Usage problems
Assign essay 4
Hmwk: Ch. 9

March

7   Writing a paper for a literature class
Essay 4 due
Writing across the curriculum
Hmwk: Ch. 10

14 Discuss topic for final exam
Review course goals, objectives
Hmwk: Outline final exam

Textbooks: *The Compact Handbook*
American Heritage Dictionary, 3e
Supplemental materials: pen drive

Suggested daily/weekly readings: *New York Times, Newsweek
Wall Street Journal*

Last day to drop class: 4 March

Attendance policy: Attendance in class is important. To that end, quizzes may NOT be made up.

Final grade:

Quizzes	20% (one per week)
Essay 1	10% (due 1/24)
Essay 2	20% (due 2/7)
Essay 3	20% (due 2/21)
Essay 4	10% (due 3/7)
Final exam	20% (3/21, 8 to 10 AM)

Figure 4.3—First Class Checklist

Prepare course outline (see Figure 4.4, page 64.)

Select text book(s)

Write behavioral objectives

Prepare laboratory manual (if a laboratory course)

Develop evaluation procedures

Develop assignments

Construct tests

Develop course web site

Prepare statement on academic honesty

Decide on office hours

Place books on reserve in library (if needed)

Develop pre-tests (if required)

Write procedures on missing tests, re-marking tests, etc.

Develop assignment hand-out

No matter how much preparation you do well ahead of your first actual class, it is still a case of "first impressions count most." So what should you do to make sure that the first class goes well?

 There are instructors who use the first class to introduce the course and themselves to the class and then finish. They don't do any teaching until the second class. Start the way you intend to continue — that is to teach.

The First Class

It is important to arrive early in the classroom, and to come fully prepared. If possible, visit the actual classroom before and figure out how to correctly use the audiovisual equipment. Make sure you know how to turn on/off the room lights, and have a working microphone if it is a large room which requires the use of an amplifier. If you intend to distribute materials to the class, have them available at the door, or distribute them during the class time.

Stand by the door of the classroom on the first day. Personally welcome each student as they arrive and hand out any printed materials that are to be distributed. Obviously, this type of welcome is easier to do with a small class, but it's worth the effort as it gives the impression that you're interested in having the students there.

At the start of a new class, I briefly introduce myself and the course, and make reference to the evaluation scheme. I then tell the students that I will be teaching this period. I give an overview of what I intend to cover (behavioral objectives, concept map etc.), and then start to teach. I teach for approximately 12-14 minutes, and then take a two-minute break (having explained its real purpose). After that, I give another mini-lecture.

I finish the class with a student activity as a way of allowing them to get to know their classmates, and to indicate that my classes involve students in their own learning.

When talking about the "Scientific Method," I use an activity which describes a particular experiment and then asks students to form small groups to work out the good and poor features of the experiment and how the experiment could be improved. I give students about ten minutes for the activity, and then ask groups to give me first, the good aspects, and then the poor aspects, and write the responses on the board. Then, I ask for ideas as to how to improve the experiment, and again note these points on the board. The class ends with a summary of what we have covered during this first class.

A first class such as this sets the scene nicely for the rest of the semester. The students will have seen how well-prepared and efficient you were, understand your teaching style, and that you involved them in a student-centered activity. A good teacher is recognized as one who is well prepared, has a good knowledge of the subject, and shows a passion for teaching and their subject and so it is important to convey these characteristics in the first class. Show your enthusiasm for teaching, your subject, and your interest in students.

Figure 4.4—Sample Course Outline

Achievement University
Basic Statistics 101 Course Outline
I. Introduction
    A. Basic statistics—use and purposes
    B. Data gathering
        1. Instruments
        2. Recorded data
        3. Machine utilization
II. Presenting Data
    A. Tables
        1. Summary tables
            a. Table elements
            b. Tables with averages
    B. Graphs
        1. Types of graphs
            a. Bar
            b. Pie chart
            c. Line graph
        2. Data presentation with graphs
    C. Frequency distributions
        1. Discrete and continuous
        2. Class intervals

III. Descriptions and Comparison of Distributions
    A. Percentiles
        1. Computation of percentile
        2. Inter-percentile range
        3. Percentile score
    B. Mean and standard deviations

        1. Computation of mean
            a. From grouped data
            b. From arbitrary origin
        2. Variance formulas
    C. Frequency distributions
        1. Measures of central tendency
        2. Symmetry and skews
        3. Bimodal distributions
IV. Predictive or Estimate Techniques
    A. Regression
        1. Graphic application
        2. Assumption of linearity
    B. Correlation
        1. Computation of correlation coefficient
        2. Reliability of measurement
    C. Circumstances affecting regression and analysis
        1. Errors of measurement
        2. Effect of range
        3. Interpretation of size
V. The Normal Curve and Statistical Inference
    A. The normal distribution
        1. Mean
        2. Standard deviation
        3. Characteristics
    B. Statistical inference
        1. Employing samples
            a. Randomness
            b. Parameters
        2. Normal distribution
            a. Standard errors
            b. Unbiased estimate
            c. Confidence interval
    C. Testing hypothesis
        1. Definition of statistical hypothesis
        2. Test of hypothesis
            a. Level of significance
            b. One-sided test
        3. Computing power of test

The Lesson Plan

A lesson plan is a must for all teachers because it acts as a reference and guide for each class meeting. A flexible lesson plan allows for discussion of appropriate current events and and provides a backup system if multimedia materials or equipment do not arrive or suffer a mechanical or electrical malfunction. The plan contains important questions and quotes from supplemental material not contained in the text, and should include definitions, comments on the purposes of the class, and student and teacher activities.

Make every effort to have lesson plans reflect your creative endeavors and unique abilities as a teacher. Often, the syllabus and to some extent the course outline are dictated to faculty. The demands for accountability and institutional goals sometimes restrict these two documents. Lesson plans, however, allow greatee flexibility and permit techniques and strategies unique to the instructor, including appropriate personal experiences and anecdotes.

After determining your objectives, you then outline the major topics that will be covered, including definitions and references to sources not in the textbook, in your daily lesson plans. Your lesson plan may include everything you need to take to the classroom such as notes, handouts, computer disks, software references, etc. (Stephan, 2000). Shown in figures 4.5 and 4.6 are examples of a lesson plan and a sample form. An effective method of planning a course is to construct a plan for each class meeting, number the lessons, place them in a loose-leaf binder, and maintain them as a record and a guide for activities.

Figure 4.5—Sample Lesson Plan

Course # and Name: Algebra 101
Date_____
Session #9
Class Objectives:
1. To demonstrate equations through the use of various expressions of equality
2. To prove equality of expressions through technique of substitution
Definitions:
1. Equation is a statement that two expressions are equal
2. Expression is a mathematical statement
3. Linear equation is equation of 1st order
Student Activities:
1. Complete sample problems in class
2. Demonstrate competence of sample by board work
Instructor Activities:
1. Demonstrate validity of solution of equations
2. Assure student understanding by personal observations by seat and board work
Major Impact:
Understand the solution of basic linear equations.
Assignment: Problems—Exercise 8, pp. 41-42.

Figure 4.6—Suggested Lesson Plan Format

Course number and Name_____Date_____
(after first page simply number chronologically)
Session #_____
Definitions to be covered_____
_____
Class objective(s)_____
_____
Student activities or exercises_____
_____
Instructor activities_____
_____
Major impact or thought_____
Assignment_____
_____

Figure 4.7—Cartoon

First Time Teacher Revelation #27

CHAPTER 5
TEACHING TECHNIQUES, INSTRUCTIONAL AIDS, TESTING

Once you have made the decision concerning your objectives for the course, the next step is to choose the instructional methods and strategies necessary to carry them out. In examining these teaching strategies and techniques, you should ask yourself the following questions:

- When should I teach by demonstration and when should I encourage students to try it themselves?

- When should I explain important topics and issues verbally and when should I prepare handouts for discussion?

- When should I lecture and when should I use question-and-answer strategies?

- When should I use audiovisual aids to support my points in discussion and lecture?

- When should I utilize multimedia technology and associated strategies to enhance my teaching?

In this chapter we will discuss some of the more common techniques, teaching aids, and evaluation procedures utilized in today's classrooms. These techniques, although not necessarily new or innovative, have proven valuable over the years to successful teachers. By utilizing a variety of teaching techniques, instructors can vary their students' learning experiences and generate excitement in the classroom.

Teaching Techniques

Successful teaching depends to a certain degree upon the initiative, creativity, and risk-taking prowess of the instructor. Even instructors with these characteristics, however, must use a variety of techniques and approaches to be successful. Some of the more common techniques used by successful teachers include:

Instructor-Based Techniques	**Student-Based Techniques**
Lectures	Active learning
Discussions	Cooperative learning
Question/answer sessions	Student panels
Demonstrations	Learning cells
Guest lecturers	Buzz groups
Quality control circles	Lab assignments

Out-of-Class Activities

Outside reading assignments
Projects
Case studies
Field trips
Journal/publication readings
Term papers/Research projects
Internet research

Traditional Instructional Aids vs. Technology-Driven Aids

CDs/DVDs/videos	Chalkboards/Whiteboards
Flipcharts	Overhead transparencies
Handouts	Computer projection
Lecture notes	Multimedia presentations
Tests and testing	

These are but some of the possible activities to facilitate classroom instruction. You might start by checking off those techniques that you have used then go on to the more detailed descriptions of these classroom activities.

Instructor-Based Techniques

The Lecture

According to Bligh (2000), so ingrained is the lecture in higher education, that over 95 percent of humanities and science professors in the U.S. use it as their main teaching method, and this in spite of all the research showing that students do not learn well in lecture situations.

A study at the University of California at Berkeley (Angelo, 1991) has shown that college students only remember 20 percent of what they hear from a traditional lecture or demonstration several days after the class. Furthermore, this study also found that, in a room full of dozens of students, fewer than 15 percent are paying attention to what is being presented at any one time during the class, not counting the first eight minutes of a class when a much higher percentage of students are following the lecture.

The major reason for this is that students do not expend much energy thinking about what is being discussed in a traditional-style presentation. Students may also be so busy writing notes (or playing on their laptops) that they don't have the time to think about what they are actually doing.

It reminds me of a cartoon I have, showing a student returning home from school and telling his father, "They don't give us time to learn anything; we have to listen to the teacher all day." How very true. This does not mean that we should suddenly abandon lectures to teach but make the best use of the time we have in a class to ensure students are actually learning. Otherwise, we might find that the following saying is all too true: "With the lecture, the information usually passes from the notes of the instructor to the notes of the students without passing through the minds of either!"

One thing that greatly influenced my own teaching when I became aware of it was the issue of student attention span in the *What's the Use of Lectures* book by Bligh (1971). The following graph shows the typical decrement curve for a person's attention to a single task over a period of time such as a lecture period.

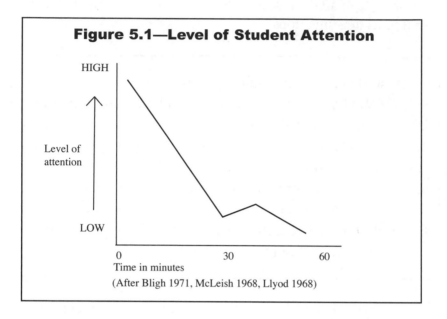

Figure 5.1—Level of Student Attention

HIGH

Level of attention

LOW

0   30   60
Time in minutes
(After Bligh 1971, McLeish 1968, Llyod 1968)

This pattern is usually displayed in the level of performance of students during a lecture. It has been suggested (McLeish 1968; Lloyd 1968) that student attention rises and falls in the last five minutes of a 55 minute lecture. Not surprisingly the student level of attention is highest at the start of a lecture but begins to decline thereafter, and around 10-20 minutes into the lecture the level of attention begins to decrease dramatically and continues to decline for the rest of the hour until the last five minutes. In fact student attention has been shown to drop off after only 10 to 15 minutes (Hartley and Davies, 1978). This suggests that the attention span of an average student might only be around 10-15 minutes during which time the most learning takes place.

Bligh (1971) notes that several studies have found a marked improvement in attention after a short break. The second graph below shows the effect of a rest or change of activity on the level of attention after a break of a few minutes. If there is such a rest period for a few minutes, when the lecture resumes, the amount of effective learning is almost as high as it was at the start of the

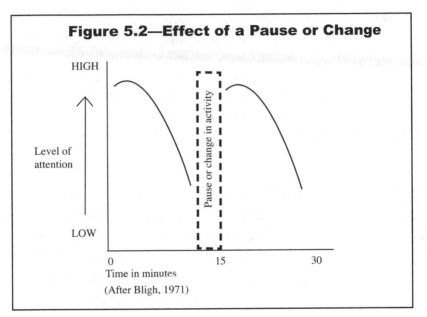

Figure 5.2—Effect of a Pause or Change

HIGH

Level of attention

LOW

Pause or change in activity

0   15   30

Time in minutes

(After Bligh, 1971)

lecture. Again, the amount of effective learning will drop off during the next part of the lecture.

A number of studies have examined the efficacy of pauses during a one-hour lecture period, and these all confirm that students are more attentive during the lecture period, and do better on subsequent tests.

Ruhl et al. (2007) point out that the pause may also benefit the lecturer since he/she may use the pauses to scan the lecture notes and, perhaps, improve the quality of his/her delivery after the pause.

Try it out for yourself! Inform your class that you will teach for 15 minutes and then take a two-minute break. During this break students should review their notes to see if there was anything

73

they didn't understand, and discuss it with a neighbor to see if the neighbor could explain it to them. If not, the student can ask questions on the material after the break. The two-minute break allows students to socialize with, and get to know their neighbors, and will give you a few minutes to get organized for the next part of the lecture.

Several years ago, to try out the strategy I used the two-minute pause with a single class during an entire semester, and when the grades for all the sections were tallied at the end of term, that section performed significantly better than all the others. And why wouldn't they? I had taught in smaller chunks of time, when student learning was most effective. Since that initial trial run, I've continued to use this technique when lecturing.

When talking to colleagues about my use of this technique, they often comment that I have *lost* four minutes of instructional time in a fifty-minute lecture! Of course, what is most important is not the *quantity* of teaching time, but the *quality* of the student learning.

It is important to point out that Bligh's graph (Figure 5.2) points to a change of activity after approximately 12-14 minutes. It follows from what we discussed in previous chapters, that good teachers employ more active techniques to allow students to become better involved in their own learning. Such activities might include solving problems you present to the class, small group discussions, demonstrations, and a variety of other techniques dealt with in this book.

It is perhaps also worth noting that Bligh (1971) reports that the rate of decrement (i.e., loss of attention) is steeper for more difficult subject matter and, therefore, the more difficult the lecture material the more frequent the pauses or variations in teaching should be. Bligh also points out that the same decrements in attention occur during the course of a day.

While some people reach their optimum level of performance during the morning, and others at midday, very few people are at their best in the afternoon. Thus, attention to lectures is more difficult in the afternoon and evening, lectures delivered at those times should be shorter, more varied, and more stimulating, should give way to small group teaching and other active methods of learning.

There are general guidelines to keep in mind when presenting the lecture. Although they are basic and well known, they are worth repeating here.

- Make certain your lecture is organized and presented in an orderly manner. Too often students are critical of instructors who appear to be rambling.

- Using illustrations throughout the lecture is an indication of a well organized lecture which the presenter is taking seriously.

- It is important that you remember to speak clearly and directly to the audience.

- Give mental breaks every ten minutes or so; that is, change the procedure by using an anecdote or activity so that the lecture is not a continuous one-way dialog.

- If you have a tendency to use distracters or mannerisms such as "you know" or "OK", be aware and avoid them.

- Use the chalk board, overhead, or any prop that you feel appropriate to enhance your lecture.

- Finally, do not hesitate to build "thinking pauses" into your lectures so your students have time mentally to catch their breath.

Discussion

Discussions are important to any interactive learning environment. They help students to formulate logic in understanding and lead to higher order learning. They allow students to identify problems and to use other members of the group as resources. This is especially important in today's diverse classroom, where older experienced adults and younger students will be sitting side by side in your class.

When stimulating class discussions, you quickly realize that this must be planned the same as any other classroom activity. Too often there is the tendency to "wait for the discussion to happen". This often leads to a lack of discussion or discussions that are not related to the topic at hand. One discussion technique is to start with a common experience. The experience might be a current event, a common problem to be solved, or a controversial issue. It may be necessary to place students in small groups, give them a topic, and have them find a solution or develop a hypothesis. Then each group can interact and question each other's findings.

Preparation for a full-class discussion requires planning as well as review of the day's topics. If the topic has been discussed with your previous classes, draw from that experience or even give some of the previous classes' conclusions and have the present class react to them. When leading the discussion, give all students the opportunity to speak. If one or two students monopolize the discussion you may wish to take their comments and ask the rest of the class to respond to them.

If there is a lull in the discussion, sometimes it is best to let the silence continue for awhile; usually there are students in the class that will feel a need to break the silence.

Urge students to talk to each other and not to you, the instructor, and if there are students who do not participate, be cognizant of that and ask them to respond to other student's comments. In leading discussions, more than any other situation in the interactive classroom, you must remember that you are a facilitator of learning and not the director of learning.

Question/Answer

Questioning students is an important tool for stimulating classroom participation and motivating students. Experienced teachers make it a rule to question as many different students as possible during a class session. Besides encouraging student participation and arousing student curiosity, questioning students is an effective way to gauge their preparation for class as well as their progress and understanding of the class topic. Eliciting answers can develop student confidence in self-expression. The right kinds of questions can also encourage higher orders of learning such as analysis, synthesis, and evaluation.

There is hardly a disadvantage associated with questioning if good judgment is exercised. Appropriate timing is important—pace questions so students have time to phrase their answers. For example, it would be unkind to continue to question a student who is embarrassed or is having difficulty responding. Such students need to be "brought along" in the classroom.

Good questioning involves several strategies:

- **Use open-ended questions when possible, that is, do not use questions that have a yes/no answer.**

- **Use questions that elicit a comment or additional queries from students, even to the point of saying to a student, "What do you think of that?"**

- **Questions should be part of the lesson plan. Prepare them ahead of time—don't wait for them to "happen."**

Different types of questions have different purposes. They are usually found in four categories: knowledge, content, discussion, and stimulation. For example,

- a **knowledge question** might be: "What is a spread-sheet?"

- a **content question** might be: "What are the functions of a spreadsheet?"

- a **discussion question** might be: "What are the advantages and disadvantages of using a spreadsheet?"

- a **stimulation question** might be: "How can spread-sheets enhance your job accuracy?" This may be followed with "Why do you think this?"

One would not normally pose questions as a form of graded evaluation because this intimidates students and typically negates the purpose of asking the question. Whenever possible, questions should be addressed to individuals by name rather than to the whole class. If your class is giving you the silent treatment, a quick question and answer can bail you out.

Another benefit to using questions and answers is the way it encourages students to ask questions of their own. Skillful questioning stimulates students to respond with questions that show higher levels of thinking.

Encouraging student questioning means eliminating any threat to the questioner. Sometimes teachers, without knowing, discourage student questioning by moving so quickly through the course material that they don't appear to have time to consider a question. Some teachers may actually say "hold your questions until the end of class." This is not only discouraging; it also runs the risk that the student will forget a question valuable to the class discussion.

Some of the techniques involved in encouraging questions from students include:

- show complete respect for any questions or comments made by students,

- specifically ask students questions during the presentation,

- use probing questions with the students,

- ask students if they need clarification on any points or issues,

- ask students to give the pros and cons of a particular issue or point, and

- have other students ask questions concerning the response.

The Demonstration

For classes that lend themselves to this technique, a demonstration is an effective way to teach skills because it combines hearing with seeing. Research shows that nearly 90 percent of learning takes place when both of these two senses are involved. Demonstration has other advantages:

- It is motivational.
- It attracts attention and can be presented to groups or to individual students.
- It is effective for large group instruction.

The demonstration is probably under-utilized as a teaching tool. To be successful, demonstration requires extensive preparation. To adequately prepare, you should simulate the demonstration prior to the class presentation. This allows you to examine the problems, be alert to possible difficulties, and even to forewarn the students that some steps are particularly difficult. Through this simple warning, the students will lend support and assist in making the demonstration successful.

Some guidelines for a successful demonstration include:

- Double-check that you have all materials and tools.
- Complete a checklist for materials and procedures as you perform the demonstration. Students can then "check" to assure correct procedure.
- State and distribute the objectives of the demonstration along with the expected outcomes.
- Have students write conclusions to the demonstration.

Although demonstrations carry the risk of failure; this is a small risk as compared to the benefits gained by showing as well as telling. Students normally will be less critical of teachers who are not successful when attempting complicated techniques. They are much more critical of boring repetitious classes.

The Guest Lecturer

In most college classrooms, guest lecturers are under-utilized. Most communities are rich with individuals who are willing, usually at no charge, to share their experiences and expertise. Our rapidly changing world makes it nearly impossible for faculty members to remain current on all issues. Inviting individuals who are on the cutting edge of changes in business, industry and community agencies to speak not only provides information but also a glimpse of the "real world" of work. Again, it is necessary to structure such a visitation so that students are aware of the objectives of the activity.

 Beware of the danger that students will become a listening audience rather than questioning participants; students need to either prepare questions prior to the visit or be given time after the guest lecturer speaks to compose questions. You should also be sure to brief the guest lecturer on the objectives and intent of the visit and to act as mediator between students and lecturer.

Quality Control Circles

Quality control circles are one of the most dynamic and interesting concepts that has evolved in the past decade. It is a management technique generally credited to the Japanese (Weimer, 1990). This technique can be very effective with adult students because it requires the involvement of employees (students) in some of the class decision-making activities. It is a relatively simple process and is especially helpful for part-time teachers who do not have daily contact with students.

During the first class session, the instructor asks for five or six volunteers to join the quality circle. The group meets periodically with the instructor, possibly during a class break or after class, to provide feedback concerning the progress of the class. The feedback might include comments concerning lecture, discussion, homework, testing, or other class activities. This process provides an ongoing feedback mechanism that involves students. It will also provide student support as you implement the circles' suggestions in the class presentation.

Student-Based Techniques

Active Learning

If you have recently read professional literature or attended faculty development workshops, you have heard the expression "active learning." You may wonder, is this strategy significantly different from learning strategies of the past? Basically, active student learning dictates that the personal learning needs of the students override the instructor/discipline-oriented learning of the past. In this scenario, the teacher develops a learning environment where students actively talk, listen and react to the course content through group activities, role playing, cooperative learning, and other student interaction techniques. The purpose of these activities is for students to apply what they are learning by sharing.

In active learning, students are no longer passive participants but become responsible for their own learning. This provides students opportunities to collaborate and cooperate with others, rather than competing. Critical thinking skills are emphasized as well as an increased opportunity for students to express their values and understanding of their culture.

As you consider these interactive student-centered techniques, you may be tempted to ask, "don't all teachers do these things?" The answer is no; regardless of the emphasis placed upon varying teaching techniques and student involvement, studies still show that the teacher does over 60 percent of the talking in class.

Active learning techniques are applicable for all disciplines. In implementing these techniques it is important to recognize that the instructor's role is as a facilitator rather than as a director of learning. The instructor as a facilitator must establish rapport with the class and encourage and stimulate student discussion. Treating students with respect and showing a sense of humor and patience will help to establish this kind of environment. Students need to understand that their questions and comments are valuable and that they will not be ridiculed for seemingly inappropriate observations or questions.

Very often nonverbal cues can be used by the instructor to relax the students. Talking directly to and walking toward the students who are raising questions or issues shows the entire class you respect them. A nod of the head or a concentrated look conveys a similar message that you are interested or understand. Moving around the room, looking relaxed and actually joining the class is another valuable nonverbal activity.

Cooperative/Collaborative Learning

Cooperative learning (also called collaborative learning), is one of the oldest educational techniques. In theory, cooperative learning brings students with differing abilities together into small groups where they teach each other the concepts of the class by reinforcing lecture and text materials. In practice, students either work on specific projects cooperatively or take selected quizzes and/or tests together. The process forces all students to become actively involved in classroom activities. Adult learners relate to cooperation in the classroom because of the cooperation required in most workplaces.

To effectively use cooperative learning techniques, you must spend considerable time structuring the situation so that each student understands their role as well as the objectives of the group.

A good cooperative learning group needs several conditions, that:

- all students must participate,

- a method to capture the individual member participation be used, and

- a written product must be the result.

For instructors, the two basic requirements for cooperative learning are thorough planning and a total commitment.

As a facilitator the instructor becomes an idea person, a resource person, a mediator (conflict resolution is as much an accomplishment in cooperative education as it is in the workplace or in life itself), and a supporter of students' efforts. Virtually all academic and technical disciplines can benefit from this technique.

Preliminary planning includes a discussion of classroom goals, specific activities that can be assigned cooperatively, and the balance sought between traditional and cooperative classroom activities. If grades are going to be assigned for group work the students must be made aware of this at the beginning of the term; the assignment of the same grade to each member of a group is the incentive needed to make cooperative learning work effectively.

The optimum size for a work group is four or five students; more students can be unwieldy while fewer opens the door to domineering students. Groups can be formed by:

- students themselves,
- the instructor assigning students to a group,
- random assignment, or
- selection based upon similar interests or specific criteria.

Typically, instructors should assign students, rather than allowing to form their own groups.

 Decided disadvantages of student-based selection are that students may choose to be with friends, thus excluding assimilation of new students into the mainstream of the class, and there may be stress in arranging groups if students do not know each other and have no basis for selection.

The benefits of cooperative learning include: adults have a vehicle to get to know others in class; attendance tends to be better (a result of a commitment to the group); improved grades due to an increased understanding of the subject matter; classroom groups lead to study groups outside of class; and students become participants in their own learning.

Instructors must regularly re-evaluate their classroom styles to accommodate changes in technology, abilities of students, and demands of students. Cooperative learning is but one of many viable strategies to encourage participation by students. Obstacles that might be encountered are: some students feel they have paid money to take the course, therefore the teacher is expected to stand in front of the class and lecture; groups may not take an assignment seriously; and some individuals may have difficulty working within a group. However, problems can be overcome by involving students in decisions regarding cooperative activities and adapting the assignments to the students in the class.

Adults are sensitive to how others view them and tend to be more candid when working in small groups; working with fellow students provides adults the opportunity to grow within the small group until they are ready to face larger groups.

The Student Panel

A student panel can be used as an alternative to lecturing by giving groups of students the opportunity to do the presenting. However, it must be structured so the specific objectives of the assignment are clearly defined prior to the panel presentation. Normally, a panel should consist of two to four members. Each member of the panel should be assigned specific topics or issues to be presented and/or defended. After the presentation, the rest of the class should be divided into discussion groups so these students can define their positions on the panel's topic. Instructors should remember to help students in developing open-ended questions for the rest of the class. A carefully structured panel is a valuable learning experience for the participants as well as the class.

The Learning Cell

In learning cells, students work in pairs to help each other learn; typically, the entire class is paired off for this activity. The pairs can work together in many different ways. It may involve an reading assignment in which the students share what they have read and then develop questions to present to one another. In this case they are demonstrating their reading comprehension and understanding of the issues while sharing their responses. Another possibility uses an open-question format where students can exercise their creativity in their responses or in a problem-solving situation. During the process the teacher moves about the room, going from pair to pair, seeking feedback and answering questions. Learning cells may be term-long assignments of students in pairs or may be assigned for a single class meeting.

Buzz Groups

As an in-class activity, the buzz group's purpose is to solve a specific problem or compare and contrast an issue. The instructor identifies the discussion topic or problem and allows students to form small groups, usually of three to five students. The students are given the freedom to develop their own discussion guidelines for reaching a solution to the issue. The solution is prepared for presentation, possibly on a flipchart or overhead transparency for the following class session. Occasionally the instructor may have a solution prepared and use it as a discussion of the differences between the student buzz groups' and the instructor's conclusions.

Buzz groups should not be confused with small group projects. Buzz groups are as a quick conclusion activity that takes 10 to 15 minutes of class time.

Out-of-Class Activities

Outside Readings/Written Assignments

Outside readings and additional assignments can be used by part-time instructors in several ways. Since neither the instructor nor the student is on campus for extensive library use, outside readings and references should be listed in the syllabus. It will aid part-time students significantly if materials and periodicals selected are available in public libraries or online. The preparation of handouts with reference numbers will also assist students. This allows students to spend their time in the library actually using the materials rather than searching for them. Again, being specific in terms of the topic and objectives (and points counted toward the grade) are necessary for a successful outside reading assignment.

The Project

Student projects are a way students can get the opportunity to learn outside the classroom. Projects may consist of in-depth research into a class topic or a community-based activity such as agency visitations, interviews, or case studies. A properly developed project should allow students to choose from a variety of related activities within their own sphere of interest. After topics are selected, instructor expectations for completion of the project should be clarified. The project should weigh significantly in the final evaluation and assignment of a grade.

The Case Study

Traditionally, case studies have been used mainly in sociology or psychology classes. The case study may, however, be used in many other disciplines. Students may be given case studies of individuals or processes in finance, investing, historic contrast, geology or other class situations. In a good case study, the instructor establishes the scenario, the objectives of the case, and the problem(s) that may be encountered. Students may then be given time to read and research the project and write their case paper or make an oral presentation which can result in student discussions to reach consensus or a conclusion. Case studies are normally assigned to individual students and not to groups.

Field Trips

Field trips should be planned so that the entire session of the field trip is on location. The class activities and trip objectives should be outlined prior to the trip. Arrange the class in small groups, specify to the students what they are to observe. At the conclusion of the visit, meet to discuss the major points observed and any conclusions to be made. The most effective field trips include credit toward the grade and require a written or oral report.

Large Group Instruction (See Chapter 8)

Although not a specific classroom technique, there are several strategies to improve large group instruction. Large classes are more impersonal and usually more difficult to teach. Successful large classes require greater preparation of materials, including more handouts and visual aids. The importance of a well-prepared lecture takes on added importance in large group instruction.

Some suggestions for easing the burden of teaching large classes include:

- **start out positively** by indicating that although large, the class is important and you are glad to be there;
- **keep a seating chart**;
- **try to learn a few student's names each day**, walk around the large classroom and try to identify students with whom you have had discussions;
- **use techniques such as buzz groups, panels, collaborative learning**—don't assume that standard strategies do not work;
- **utilize the cell or partner format.** In a class of 100, utilizing cells reduces responses to 50, or utilize cooperative learning strategies. Again, in a class of 100, using this technique will reduce the class to the equivalent of 20 students;
- **share your research, anecdotes, and background.** With a large class, chances are that someone in your class may have had similar experiences and might be willing to share them;
- **utilize the overhead projector, videos, and all types of technology** to vary the teaching activities;
- **use technology to communicate with your students.** Use your e-mail to share pertinent questions with all students. You can also use Twitter, or create a chatroom, bulletin board. Be sure to share the responses with the rest of your class;
- **involve students** by asking for a show of hands or holding up colored cards (green for "I understand," red for "I don't understand");
- **have students write a brief response** paragraph to major questions and have them hand it in;

- **at the end of class ask students to drop a written question** to you on the way out, and at the beginning of the next class use the question to commence discussions;

- **keep students involved by giving short quizzes** (maybe ungraded) and use a show of hands to get feedback on the correct responses;

- **clearly identify major points and questions**;

- **arrange a 20-minute discussion group** before and/ or after class for students who are having trouble in a large group setting; and

- **move around**—up the aisles and around the room as you lecture.

It is important that active techniques be utilized in large classes. Many teachers have a tendency to "give up" the interactive student responses, thinking that it is impossible in large group instruction.

Instructional Aids

Technology provides a plethora of tools for use in the classroom, as well for use communicating with students outside of class. The comprehensive multimedia presentation requiring the faculty member to make use of available training and support materials, such as computer hardware and software, is described in greater detail in Chapter 7. A brief review of the traditional instructional aids follows.

Overhead Transparencies

The overhead projector has become one of the most popular support tools in education because it allows instructors to face the class while showing images on the screen using normal room lighting. Overhead projectors are inexpensive and are usually readily available from the academic division office or the audio-visual department. Some projectors are equipped with a roll that provides a continuous writing surface. This enables the retention of information on the roll in the event students later wish to discuss specific points and is especially useful in mathematics, engineering, etc. classes.

There is no limit to the artistic excellence that can be produced on a transparency. Many faculty members easily prepare their own transparencies. Transparencies may be typewritten, handwritten, computer-generated, or drawn on standard-size plain white paper and instantaneously produced on a standard copier. Many times it is worth the extra effort to make a professional-looking overhead transparency. They are easily maintained, durable, and thus can be a permanent part of future presentations.

CD/DVD

Probably the most effective modern instructional aid is the CD/DVD. With the reduction in cost of recorders and the discs, the possibilities for expanded use are nearly endless. Most institutions now have equipment for instructors who wish to develop their own video clips as well as a library of CD/DVDs that may be applicable to your class. CDs/DVDs are not only attention getters, but provide the opportunity for direct student involvement when students produce their own video/audio clips. However, instructors must indicate to the students the objectives behind any video assignments, and combine the video with discussion, a written report, or other activity.

Flipchart

A commonly used visual aid for business seminars is a simple flipchart. When adapted to the classroom, the flipchart has many advantages over a chalkboard or overhead projector. The flipchart, a large tablet with pages that can be flipped vertically, is especially useful for small groups to record their discussions and conclusions. Instructors can record major points of a presentation and have room to add notes, descriptions, or comments. The information can then be retained by tearing off the page and taping it to the wall for future reference. A flipchart and felt-tip pen can be one of the most effective tools in the active classroom.

NOTE: When planning on an instructional aid, be sure you have all the equipment you require before the class begins whether it's chalk, markers, flipchart easels, masking tape, or the computer to project your materials.

Handouts

Although sometimes overused, handouts are still a valuable instrument for instructors. Modern copy technology along with computers and printers make preparing and updating easy. Handouts should be used for material that students will need for reference, such as important definitions, computations, or position statements for discussion. Handouts for lecture purposes should contain only an outline of the material discussed with space for students to add their own comments.

A serious note of caution: be careful of copyright violations! Your supervisor or department head should be able to provide you with the Fair Use guidelines you will need to follow.

Tests and Testing

There are multiple reasons for testing students. First and foremost is the evaluation to assist in the assignment for the total grade. In addition, however, tests serve multiple purposes. Testing communicates to the instructor if the course objectives are being met and to what degree. Of equal importance, tests are used as an instructional tool and a learning device for students. When tests are used for evaluation you must be careful to inform the students at the beginning of the class of the testing procedure, when they will be given, and the criteria upon which they will be based. Too often students are overheard criticizing their instructors with, "they didn't test over what they talked about in class."

Test/Question Types

The major types of tests used in college classes are: essay, multiple choice, and recall. In special circumstances, performance, oral, and short answer tests may also be utilized.

Essay Tests/Questions. Essay tests are still one of the most popular of colleges tests. They are effective at any level of the learning hierarchy. Although essay tests require considerable time for students to respond, they do give an in-depth perspective of overall student ability. There are several factors to remember when writing test questions that require essay answers. Most important is that essay questions should be related to the written course objectives. They should incorporate a significant amount of content, including discussion, contrasting, comparing, etc. Finally, you must be certain that in terms of vocabulary, content, and subject covered, the student has sufficient background to respond adequately to the question being asked and that the question is not ambiguous or deceptive.

Grading essay questions presents the greatest problem. You must keep in mind that essay questions are asking students to be objective, yet justify their answers. The appropriate way to judge an essay response is to list important items for the response and prioritize them, assigning more points to the highest priority. Assigning points to the prioritized criteria will then lead to a degree of grading objectivity.

 You must be cautious, however, that essay questions do not ask for student opinions since it's impossible to assign evaluation points to opinions.

Multiple Choice Tests/Questions. With the advent of computerized scoring and large classes, multiple choice tests probably are the most used tests in college classrooms today. They not only are efficient in terms of time consumed, but with the use of item analysis, can determine question validity.

The development of multiple choice questions is not a simple matter. The actual construction of the multiple choice tests has several general guidelines, including:

- do not include answers that are obviously correct or incorrect, including impossible responses or distracters,
- be sure the correct answers are scattered throughout the response mechanism,
- provide four possible responses to minimize the guess factor,
- do not use "all of the above" or "none of the above,"
- do not use the terms never, always, likely, or similar adjectives that may divert the meaning for the student,
- be consistent with the format so that students are not confused with wording or punctuation changes, and
- keep choices approximately the same length since incorrect answers are frequently shorter than correct ones.

Disadvantages of multiple choice tests are: they often test on only the knowledge level rather analysis and synthesis; they provide opportunity for guessing; and they depend primarily on recall and memory.

Recall and Completion Tests/Questions. Recall items may be posed as simple questions, completion, or brief response. Used too often, these tests tend to encourage students to memorize rather than understand. There are, however, advantages to recall tests. They are relatively simple to grade and construct; they can address a broad field of content; and they require specific recall rather than guessing or rationalization.

Some suggestions for developing recall questions are:

- Give information concerning the answer prior to the answer blank,
- Qualify information so students are clear about the response,
- Include responses at the analysis and synthesis level,
- Pose questions so that only one correct response is usable,
- Allow sufficient and equal space for the response,
- Avoid patterns of responses,
- Avoid direct quotes, and
- Avoid specific descriptors or adjectives.

 True/false questions are not commonly used at the college level any longer. Although they may have their place in a sampling of student responses or learning activity, they generally are not accepted as being objective or valid.

Assigning Grades

The Basics

Grading students is probably the most difficult task for faculty. All of the elements of teaching (preparation, presentation, and student activity) are reflected in the grading process. In addition, in an era of accountability, teachers are sometimes called upon to justify grades with documentation. Thus the establishment of firm criteria for grading is necessary. There are some general rules that are helpful in establishing the grading process. They are as follows:

- Communicate criteria clearly to the students.
- Include criteria other than test scores.
- Avoid irrelevant factors such as attendance and tardiness in the grading criteria.
- Place grading criteria carefully throughout the course.
- Weigh grading criteria carefully and always have a plan.
- Grade students on their achievement.

Many years ago, teachers used the technique of "grading on the curve." This placed students in competition with each other rather than cooperating in the learning experience. The practice has been abandoned in the modern classroom.

Evaluation Plan

In order to clearly delineate criteria for assignment of grades, it is helpful if you first develop an evaluation plan. An evaluation plan is a very simple device developed in a short worksheet form. The plan contains all of the factors that apply to the evaluation of the students. Across from these factors is listed a percentage of weight that will be assigned to various factors. A third column indicates the points received for each factor. A sample plan is shown in the figure 5.3 on the following page.

Figure 5.3—Evaluation Plan

Grade Factors	Percentage of Final Grade	Possible Points	Points Received
Tests	60%	90	————
Paper	20%	30	————
Project	10%	10	————
Class Participation	10%	15	————
TOTALS	100%	145	————

Note that this type of plan allows you the freedom to assign any number of points to any criteria or activity because the final percentage will always come out to 100 percent.

 This documentation clearly indicates to the students the process by which evaluation is conducted in a businesslike and professional manner. Once the evaluation plan is completed, it is essential that it be included in the course syllabus since that is the official document of the course.

CHAPTER 6
STUDENT ENGAGEMENT—WHY IT MATTERS

This chapter is contributed by Dr. Bruce A. Johnson, who originally wrote the materials for his blog on AdjunctNation.com. Dr. Johnson throughout his entire career has been involved in many forms of adult education, including teaching, training, human resource development, coaching, and mentoring. Dr. Johnson has completed a master's in Business Administration and a Ph.D. in the field of adult education. Presently Dr. Johnson works as an online adjunct instructor, faculty developmental workshop facilitator, and faculty mentor.

Student Retention—Why It Matters

When you hear the phrase student retention, what comes to mind? Is it a set of numbers that the school hopes to achieve? Is it something to be addressed from a school-wide perspective, which is beyond your control? Or do you consider the impact that you have upon student retention for the school? It is easy to view student retention, student satisfaction, and student persistence as a responsibility of the school that should be addressed through initiatives, proper course development, student support, and other relative issues. While it is important for any school to be concerned about the rate of retention and the policies that support student satisfaction, it is just as important to remember that instructors represent the school through their classroom interactions with students.

Students interact with a learning environment that is created by the instructor and supported by the school. If students do not have a positive experience or meaningful classroom interactions they are likely to develop a negative perception about the school, which can also have a direct bearing on their decision to continue with their degree program. Student retention begins with the initial instructor that is assigned for the very first course and continues with each subsequent instructor, one class at a time. It is more than a student feeling happy about their decision to attend the school; it is about relationships that are developed, expectations that are addressed, and developmental needs being met. Students make the initial decision and instructors reaffirm or negate that choice through their classroom instruction.

Students Make the First Choice

When a student decides to attend a particular school, it is often because they are interested in a specific degree program and they have personal or professional needs that need to be met. As a means of attracting new students, schools will promote resources, services, features, and other benefits offered. Students often make an initial decision based upon their expectations of what they hope to receive, achieve, and learn by attaining their degree. Learning about the reality of these expectations occurs when students begin their classes.

Instructors Reaffirm or Negate that Choice

An instructor helps students confirm, discard, or adapt their expectations about the process of learning through the environment they create. This includes all aspects of classroom facilitation, including discussions, working relationships, and the feedback provided. When an instructor is responsive to the need of their students, students are likely to believe their developmental needs can be met. Instructors that successfully create a meaningful learning environment encourage students to maintain continued progress, which results in retention. The goal is not just to keep students in their degree programs, but to improve educational outcomes — where students create knowledge and develop skill sets through their active participation in the process of learning. Student retention further becomes an issue of persistence because they may face challenges throughout their academic journey, including such issues as time management, self-motivation, and skill set development.

Retention is More than Numbers

There are many components to student retention and from a developmental perspective one of the most important issues is sustained growth—the development of skill sets and the acquisition of knowledge on the part of each student. From the student's perspective, there is a perception of rewards that are received, and an expected return on investment. Student retention involves a culmination of experiences, which means they are motivated to continue and they are having positive experiences and interactions with their instructors and the learning environment.

Negative interactions with instructors may have a direct impact on the perception students develop about the school overall. Students will either persist, because of the commitment made to complete their degree program, or they will leave out of frustration and resentment.

 While an instructor may not be able to predict how students will react to their particular method of classroom facilitation; their attitude towards students and the conditions they create in the classroom will often determine if students continue their program. Student retention is not exclusively about numbers, it is the essence of interactions developed throughout the duration of the class. It all begins with the instructor.

Student Engagement 101

As an instructor do you expect that your students will be active and present in the class? The level of a student's involvement in the class and the learning process are often assessed by his or her performance and the work product submitted; however, does active involvement equal engagement in the class? What does student engagement mean to you and to your class? Instructors who understand the process of engagement, can encourage students to become involved in the class, which in turn may lead to improved classroom and individual performance.

Defining Student Engagement

Engagement is an action-based state that consists of the time, energy, and effort that the student devotes to his or her class. The process of being engaged in the class involves more than the student just getting by in his or her class or doing the minimum required to pass the course. When a student is engaged in the class they are devoting the time necessary to become an active participant in the process of learning and their attention is focused on the course.

A student may consciously think about being engaged in the class or it may occur as a reaction to specific requirements, such as a participation requirement or a group project. It is possible for the level of a student's engagement to frequently change, depending upon the interactions and experiences with other students and the instructor. For example, if the student is feeling confident with her/his progress and abilities, that positive emotion can enhance engagement. In contrast, if the student feels discouraged engagement and progress may diminish.

 Adam Fletcher (2009) has found that "student engagement is increasingly seen as an indicator of successful classroom instruction."

Engagement may be enhanced or reduced if there is a feeling of being disconnected from the class or the instructor. Students who experience negative interactions may retreat from the class or withdraw their active engagement from the class as a reaction or retaliation for what they have experienced or how they have perceived a particular incident.

When adults experience engagement in what they are doing they are devoting their full attention to the task and they are enthusiastically involved, highly interested, and experiencing positive emotions. Active engagement can lead to increased participation in the class discussions, which is a gauge that instructors often used to measure the level of a student's participation.

The Instructor's Role in Student Engagement

The process of learning itself may produce emotional reactions that can influence engagement. If an instructor encourages students to utilize critical thinking and reflection students are likely to experience a range of emotions while exploring their opinions, ideas and belief systems. The process of critical self-examination can happen while the student is working on his or her own or during classroom discussions, emphasizing the need for instructors to provide support and guidance. Instructors have an ability to establish classroom conditions that encourage positive interactions in a productive, respectful environment. When students feel positive emotions and have experiences that produce positive emotions they are likely to be fully engaged in the learning process and actively present in the class.

The instructor's level of engagement has a direct impact on a student's level of engagement. A student who believes their instructor is present in his or her class will be more active and engaged in the class as well. Students also react to their instructor's ongoing engagement in the class. The Maryville University web site informs students that they will discover "enthusiastic professors with impressive academic credentials and professional experience." When instructors demonstrate a high level of enthusiasm as they engage in the class, it provides an example for students to follow.

Dr. Richard D. Jones (2008) notes that "it is easy to observe the lack of student engagement when students are slouched in their chairs and not listening to the teacher or participating in the discussion." From the instructor's perspective, adult learner engagement may be observed but not measured as the instructor is often focused on the required assignments, class discussions, and administrative aspects of classroom facilitation. In addition, many classroom assessments are designed to measure performance and progress towards meeting the required learning objectives rather than the level of engagement. Because student assessments are performance driven, engagement often becomes a criteria that is considered but not measured.

It is possible that increased engagement will have a positive impact on individual and classroom performance; therefore, instructors should consider methods of engaging students in the class.

Encouraging Student Engagement

Factors that frequently influence student engagement in any classroom environment include family and career responsibilities, along with their attitude, prior class experiences, and perceptions about the class, their instructor, and the ability of the course to meet their needs. An instructor can take a pro-active approach and encourage student engagement through the following techniques.

Students who have negative interactions with their instructor or other students may retreat from the class or withdraw their active engagement from the class in retaliation for what they have experienced or how they have perceived a particular incident. As noted within the article "Drivers of Persistence" by the New England Literacy Resource Center, "it is human nature that when we feel welcomed, respected, and develop a sense of belonging, we are more apt to return to the setting or endeavor than when those factors are not present." Instructors set the overall tone from the first day of class and every subsequent interaction with their students.

Dr. Richard Jones (2008) reminds instructors that "relevance can help create conditions and motivation necessary for students to make the personal investment required for rigorous work or optimal learning," and that "students invest more of themselves, work harder, and learn better when the topic is interesting and connected to something that they already know." Class discussions provide an opportunity to add relevance as an instructor can connect students to the course topics by sharing real world examples, their own experiences, and supplemental resources that bring the course topics to life.

Tristan de Frondeville (2009) notes that "although it may take years to develop the repertoire of skills and lessons that enable you to permanently create this active-learning environment, you can begin by discerning which activities truly engage your students." If a learning activity does not generate students' interest then it's time to consider revising or eliminating that activity. While it's not possible to create excitement and enthusiasm for every class activity and assignment it is important to consider if the activities are busy work or something relevant to the learning objectives and have a potential to enhance the process of learning.

Demonstrate Engagement for Your Students

It is possible to model active engagement in the class with daily participation postings, availability to address questions and concerns, and frequent communication. Chris Palmer (2009) believes that instructors should "convey your passion and enthusiasm for the subject" and as a result "when students see their professor's passion, they want to participate." In a traditional classroom environment students physically observe their instructor's involvement in the class, along with their enthusiasm and passion. For the online classroom those characteristics are demonstrated through discussion boards and written communication.

Other Factors Related to Student Engagement

Adam Fletcher (2009) has conducted a literature review of this topic and listed "five indicators for student engagement in college," which include "the level of academic challenge, active and collaborative learning, student-faculty interaction, enriching education experiences and a supportive learning environment." One method of addressing this list of indicators is to allow students to make choices concerning their assignments or involvement with the class as a means of encouraging them to feel that they had a choice in their level of engagement. For example, students could receive a list of possible topics for an assignment and choose one that is of interest to them. Another method of connecting with students in a way that encourages engagement is to provide written feedback each week about the student's overall progress and discuss specific resources that address their developmental needs.

Let's consider the questions posed in this chapter. Does active involvement equal engagement? Engagement is an action-based state. If the students are actively involved in the class through their participation in discussions and the submission of assignments that demonstrate progress throughout the class it is likely that instructors will view this level of involvement as engagement in the class.

What does student engagement mean to you and to your class? Instructors have the ability to influence student engagement in the class by providing support and guidance, being actively present in the class, developing meaningful interactions, and demonstrating engagement through their participation, passion, and enthusiasm. The goal is to create a learning environment that encourages students to be involved, because students who are highly motivated to participate in the learning process are likely to also be engaged in the class.

CHAPTER 7
COMMUNICATING WITH STUDENTS

Keep Information Flowing

There are, of course, a number of different methods of communication based on the computer, beginning with e-mail. However, e-mail is not always the best medium for communications between instructors and whole classes of students. E-mail should be reserved for messages of a personal nature between an instructor and the student. Messages from an instructor to a whole class or between class members are better done through a class listserv or web forum. Questions about the course content may be posted on the web forum, and the instructor (or other student) response is posted for all to see. Class notices, such as times and places of exams etc., may also be posted in this way. A web forum may also be used for class discussions on topics of interest. There are a number of other computer-based modes of communication including weblogs (blogs) and Twitter.

Blogs

"A blog is a frequently updated web site consisting of dated entries called posts (including text, images, media objects, and data) arranged in reverse chronological order so the most recent entry appears first" (Brownstein and Klein, 2006).

Brownstein and Klein point out that blogs may be used as virtual environments, where all students may participate in critical discourse on scientific topics. In many ways blogs are similar to web forum postings. Since blogs are well-accepted methods for communicating one's thoughts or ideas, or responding to other people's postings, they are now being used by many college and university professors, although because of their fairly recent appearance on the scene there is little research published on their uses and their effect on student learning.

Brownstein and Klein (2006) write that, "Blogging gives voice to students who often feel uncomfortable speaking up in class and can have a powerful impact on a greater number of students in the classroom as it supports more learning styles." They have identified a noticeable change in the quality and quantity of learning taking place in the classroom since introducing blogs. In particular, the focus has moved from "what" to "why."

Blogs then offer another format for communications in a classroom, and given their current popularity in the Internet world will continue to be electronic communication tools of use in teaching.

Twitter

The web site Twitter.com is a more recent communication tool, similar to blogs, but one which limits posts (called "tweets") to just 140 characters. This tool, like blogs, has potential in teaching and learning, although the limited length of responses does not allow for detailed discussions. However, a recent study at the University of Leicester in the UK discovered that tweeting helped:

develop peer support among students,

develop personal learning networks, and

students to arrange social meetings.

The researchers also found that Twitter was very attractive as a data collection tool for assessing and recording the student experience, with a wide range of free and increasingly sophisticated on-line analysis tools (Cann et al., 2009).

Social Networking Sites

Sites such as YouTube, Facebook and MySpace are popular social networking sites. While these sites have a potential for use in education settings, it is not clear that they have immediate applications to teaching. However a number of instructors do use video clips which are posted on YouTube in their lectures, and it's possible to maintain pages on Facebook and MySpace for use by students in their classes to communicate with other classmates and the instructor.

Learning Management Systems

There are a number of different companies marketing learning management software, including Desire2Learn and Blackboard. Usually, the individual college or university has a license for all of the campus so the instructor may not have a choice as to which system to use. These systems have a number of different components including:

- posting class notes/videos

- links to external Web sites

- class web forum

- e-mail to instructor

- posting class notices

- example tests

- class marks register

- links to other educational software packages such as Second Life, blogs etc.

Learning management systems offer the ability to post lecture notes, PowerPoint slides, videos, class announcements, have students submit assignments electronically, to maintain class marks (which individual students can access to find out their own test scores, etc.), and to post on-line tests. Training is required to use such systems.

Second Life

"Second Life is a free on-line multi-user virtual environment (MUVE) that allows users to meet in virtual space, build and manipulate virtual objects, and converse via text or voice over internet protocol (VoIP)" (Atkinson, Wilson and Kidd, 2008).

Second Life allows for the creation of virtual classes where each user assumes a virtual, identity, an avatar, which can be controlled by the user. Since students in a class can have their own avatars, the student remains anonymous. This allows students who are quiet in a live, on-campus class, to use their avatar to ask questions, make statements, and join in discussions which they might not do in on-campus classes. Second Life may be used as an adjunct to a lecture class or as a distance education course. The software may also be used to create three-dimensional simulations, models, demonstrations which students can manipulate, interact with, or store for later use (Atkinson, Wilson and Kidd, 2008). "Different campuses host different types of events, such as scheduled lectures, media screenings, theatrical productions, labs and virtual office hours. Practically anything possible in real life is possible in SL" (Atkinson, Wilson and Kidd, 2008).

This particular application, then, offers an interesting alternative to live classes in the field of simulations whereby students, and instructors, can assume virtual, anonymous, personalities. At the present time, hundreds of North American colleges and universities use Second Life.

Student Response Systems

One problem associated with large classes particularly, is gauging student understanding of the material presented. While some students will ask questions about material they do not understand, it is usually only when marking tests and examinations that the instructor can see whether students really have understood the material presented in class. The recent advent of electronic clickers now presents an opportunity for instructors to check during class on whether or not students understand the material being presented. Clickers present us with a new, instantaneous feedback system. Herreid (2006) writes that, "They provide instant feedback to students and faculty regardless of the size of the class, and have a clear value in socialization, making impersonal classes more intimate. The technology also seems to resonate with students fascination with interactive media."

Clickers are like television remote controls, with numbered buttons that students can push to give an answer, usually to a multiple choice question. Each student's response is transmitted to a receiver which picks them up and feeds the response into a computer. The class results can be viewed by the instructor on the computer screen. The instructor can quickly gauge the level of understanding of the students and can re-teach the material if the clicker responses indicate a less than ideal understanding of the material. Herreid (2006) points out that, "Research on various forms of instructional feedback, all of which can be provided by clicker systems, has indicated direct relationships between feedback and improved student learning (Guthrie and Carlin, 2004)."

Duncan (2005) lists eleven ways in which instructors can use clickers:

- to measure what students know prior to instruction;

- to measure student attitudes;

- to find out if students have done the reading;

- to get students to confront misconceptions;

- to transform demonstrations;

- to increase students' retention of the material they have been taught;

- to test students' understanding;

- to make some kinds of assessment easier;

- to facilitate testing of conceptual material;

- to facilitate discussion and peer instruction; and

- to increase class attendance.

Textbooks often come bundled with electronic clickers so textbook choice may determine which type is used.

Even though there are only a few published assessments of clicker use, because of their novelty, Herreid (2006) writes that,

- student enthusiasm for clickers is high;

- student attendance is strikingly improved, changing from below 50 percent in the lecture method to over 80 percent when clickers are used;

- student learning appears to be improved;

- faculty enthusiasm is high; and

- student apathy is much less evident.

While there are some disadvantages of clickers (cost, steep learning curve for faculty etc.) Herreid (2006) concludes that these are minor when compared to their advantages.

If you don't have access to electronic clickers don't despair. You can get most of the advantages of them using non-electronic response systems. I have seen paper/cardboard cubes with different letters and/or colors on each side used to the same effect. When the instructor poses a question, students show (to the instructor) the side of the cube which displays their chosen response. If colored cube sides are used the instructor can quickly estimate how many members of the class have answered the question correctly, and then decide whether to move on to new material or to go over the previous material again.

CHAPTER 8
ONLINE RESEARCH

Finding Information Online

The rapid growth of the Internet has made finding reliable, credible information more challenging for the teacher and student. While there is a dizzying array of information available on virtually any topic, just try to find it. A simple search for a key word or name turns up far too many web sites to be useful; "Martin Luther King," for example, can return upwards of two million results. Among the results were web sites related to a range of items including the holiday, memorial library, and speeches devoted to Martin Luther King. While it might be possible that the first few results listed are the pages sought, the greater likelihood is that the search will result in more frustration than desired information. Instructors can and should address this problem while helping students learn better ways for doing online research.

As with other kinds of information searches, Web-based research follows the usual processes of search and find, evaluate and verify, followed by appropriate use and citation.

One search strategy uses well-established sites that have collected information resources into a kind of data warehouse of other previewed web sites. These core sites may be owned and maintained by non-profit educational institutions (often a university), non-profit organizations (**http://www.merlot.org**, for example) or for-profit corporations (such as **http://www. Proquestk12.com**). One highly recommended site is the World

Lecture Hall at the University of Texas: **http://WLH.webhost. utexas.edu**. As noted at their web site, "Welcome to World Lecture Hall, your entry point to free online course materials from around the world." A common feature of these warehouse sites is that they collect materials and web sites, organize them into discrete categories and provide tools that enable users to locate resources within the site.

General Search Engines

Another search strategy uses specialized search software or search engines. Whether proprietary or in the public domain, search engines try to find and index as many web sites and web pages as possible. Various search engines will boast about the number of sites in their indexing; others may claim an advantage based on their speed and search accuracy. The search indexing offered by the various search engines tends to be based on specific Web site characteristics, including unique key words, combinations of words, searching for particular fields of information, and limiting factors (boolean searches). No single search engine is able to index a very large portion of the Web, and none can find specific kinds of information that are behind some kind of entry portal (sites which require a searcher to log in). The content of specially formatted documents, such as Adobe PDF documents, is not searched even when the document itself is available on the Web. Understanding the features of several search engines will help students learn to use each for particular purposes.

The more common general search engines include:

> Google—**www.google.com**—a large index that includes the Web sites of many organizations; fast; uses – and/ or OR boolean operators; can limit search by language and domain.

> Bing—**www.Bing.com**—a very large index with powerful and unique searching capabilities; boolean searching with extensive language search limits.

Yahoo—**www.Yahoo.com**—a very large index; among the fastest; uses some boolean operators; can limit search by language and domain; searches for multimedia.

Ask—**www.ask.com**—a search engine launched in 1997. Instead of a user entering keywords into the form, this engine returns web pages based on a question asked by the user. The site can be used like a more traditional search engine if you prefer.

Exercises in searching for information can provide a fun and useful way for instructors to include Internet researching into the context of a class. Instructors can develop elementary levels of familiarity by using exercises that ask students to find a variety of kinds of information and web sites—a Web scavenger hunt. Students can work in small teams or individually and can report back on their success at finding certain kinds of data. In addition to easily found responses, ("At which web site would you be most likely to find information related to federal oversight of water quality?"), students can be asked to make qualitative choices as a part of this assignment, ("At which web sites would you find the most useful information related to the disputes over water quality in the Rio Grande water basin?")

 One good search practice limits the search to specified URL domains and to make use of vertical search engines. In this way the student can have some greater confidence that the material on population statistics, for example, from a web site with the URL <.gov>, is probably reliable and based on governmental census data.

Evaluating the quality of information and verifying the accuracy of the materials online represents a major issue for teaching using the Web. Even if students can find information, the real question is whether the information is useful and/or valid. Anyone can put information out online—and usually does; there is no requirement that it be validated in the same way information published in a reviewed journal. One way to address this is to use sites that are reviewed, such as sites of major academic journals or full-text databases of various journals.

Veritical Search Engines

A vertical search engine, as distinct from a general web search engine, focuses on a specific segment of online content. The vertical content area may be based on topicality, media type, or genre of content. Common verticals include education, legal information, medical information, and books/literature.

Vertical search engines offers several potential benefits over general search engines:

- Greater precision due to limited scope

- Leverage domain info. including taxonomies and ontologies

- Support specific unique user tasks

Several vertical search engines that are useful for the college faculty member are:

http://books.google.com/ Google Book Search allows searches of the world's largest index of books.

http://scienceresearch.com/scienceresearch/ ScienceResearch.com is a free deep web search engine that uses advanced "federated search technology" to return high quality results.

http://www.researchpaper.com Source of topics and ideas for student research.

http://www.loc.gov Library of Congress web site; key site for governmental data.

http://scholar.google.com/ Google Scholar provides a simple way to broadly search for scholarly literature.

http://www.emtech.net/learning_styles.html Bibliography and collection of URLs related to learning styles.

Evaluating the Reliability of Online Information

Four criteria for evaluating web pages and the information listed there, includes:

- **Who is the author?** Check the accuracy of Web documents by making sure that a name and affiliation is listed. Is there an e-mail address listed that can be used to follow up on the information? Is this person qualified to provide the information on the web site? Why was this web site created? Does it have an educational or commercial function?

- **What are the credentials of the author?** What is the authority of the web site? What is the URL domain? Is the domain from an educational institution (.edu), governmental entity (.gov), organizational group (.org), or business (.com/.biz)? Are there citations for the data presented?

- **How objective is the material presented?** Try to determine if there is a hidden agenda or commercial purpose to the information. Ask why and for whom the web page was created. One clue could be the detail of the information. What kinds of sources are cited for the data presented?

- **How current and up-to-date is the information presented?** Find out when the document was created or when it was last updated. Are there any dead links on the page? If so, this is a clue that the page has not changed recently and might indicate that the information on the page is outdated.

The appropriate use of Web information is specific to the course of study and the particular instructor (keyed to pedagogy). What is important here is that the instructor incorporate the use of search techniques with the class, instruct students in evaluation and verification of the information contained in the web sites, and finally, ensure that students appropriately cite any information found on the Web.

CHAPTER 9
TEACHING LARGE CLASSES

It is almost inevitable that teaching undergraduate courses, particularly at the introductory levels, also means teaching large classes on most college and university campuses. There is a significant difference between the way in which, say, a large class of 300 is taught as compared with a class of 30 or 50.

Teaching a large class is not just a matter of teaching more students at the same time, for the larger class is taught in a larger room with fixed seating, and the extra numbers of students makes seemingly simple things such as handing back test papers and assignments much more time-consuming. In addition to these problems, one can add a further dimension, that of students feeling anonymous, and being less likely to contribute to class discussions.

In their study of large classes Wulff et al. (1987) noted that students commented on the impersonal nature of such classes which led to decreased motivation. A third factor, according to Wulff et al. (1987) was an increase in noise and distractions ("Rude people who come late, leave early, or sit and talk to their buddies."). Cooper and Robinson (2000) write, "It is a sad commentary on our universities that the least engaging class sizes and the least involving pedagogy is foisted upon the students at the most pivotal time of their undergraduate careers: when they are beginning college."

Large class size, then, brings at least three sets of problems with which to deal, namely a more challenging teaching environment, more time-consuming administrative tasks, and a large anonymous, less involved audience. This chapter will give you some ideas as to how to tackle these challenges, and some practical examples of how to teach large undergraduate classes.

Syllabus

Lewis (1994) writes that the syllabus becomes a very important document in teaching large classes.

 When Erikson and Strommer (1991) asked students at the end of their freshman year about what instructors might have done to help them, one of the three most frequent responses was to "provide a better syllabus." (See figure 4.2)

The Lecture Hall

A large lecture hall is quite different from the average small classroom. This is why you should visit the designated lecture room ahead of the first class to get acquainted with the room. In most such venues, one's voice needs assistance to be projected to the back of the room, and so most lecture theatres are fitted with microphones, amplifiers, and speakers. In all probability, portable microphones will not be left in the room between classes (they have a tendency to "disappear") and will have to be collected from another location prior to the class. If you are using a portable microphone, remember to check the "low battery" warning light — it's important that your microphone not die on you mid-lecture.

Lewis (1994) suggests that you write something on the chalkboard, and then go to the back of the class to see if you can read it from there. Get used to writing large – 3 inches (8 centimeters) is about the *smallest* you can get away with in a lecture theatre situation. Similarly, if you use an overhead projector (still a useful piece of equipment even though it is an "older" technology), or even PowerPoint slides, try to use a font and size which can be read easily, even in the back row.

Next, find out where the light switches and dimmers are. Check to find out where other relevant controls are positioned (speaker volume control, electronically operated screen, etc.).

Is your lecture hall equipped as electronic teaching room containing a computer, a projector CD/DVD player, Internet access, and a visual presenter? If so, arrange for training in the use of all of the equipment provided.

You should also make certain that the appropriate software is on the computer to run your program. More than once I have checked everything else worked before a lecture or presentation only to find that the correct software was not on the computer to run one of my programs. One of the most useful pieces of equipment in large lecture rooms is the visual presenter. This piece of equipment does away with the need to produce overhead transparencies.

With one of these electronic cameras you can project directly from the typed page without the additional step of producing costly overheads. Since the camera can also zoom in and out, one can even project directly from the printed page in a textbook or journal and use the zoom to magnify the image. I have even projected 35 mm color slides (rapidly becoming another obsolete technology) using the camera. Most instructors use PowerPoint (or an equivalent software package) to project their notes, pictures and graphics.

Administration

Large classes can also be very time-consuming due simply to the large number of people in the class. For example, in a small class of, say 40 students, you could hand back marked tests and assignments by calling out the names of each of the students. Try handing back 200 papers that way! It would take most, if not all, of the class period just to hand back the papers. So how best to deal with collecting and distributing tests and assignments?

Ask student to place completed papers in piles marked in alphabetical order. Return the marked papers in a similar fashion, asking the students to come and pick up their papers at the end of the class.

Don't hand back tests or papers during your teaching time in class. Students will be distracted by the materials.

Lewis (1994) suggests that the following areas are ones in which an instructor may wish to consider streamlining:

1. Developing and duplicating handouts, exams and homework problems;

2. Handling out and collecting those handouts, exams, and homework problems;

3. Grading homework and exams;

4. Keeping track of several hundred student grades;

5. Providing timely feedback to students;

6. Getting questions from students and providing them with answers;

7. Managing office hours.

Teaching

Teaching a large class in a lecture theatre can bring problems of interactivity with students. Yazedjian and Kolkhorst point (2007) point out that, "Students who believe they are anonymous often feel less personally responsible for learning, are less motivated to learn, and are less likely to attend class (Cooper and Robinson 2000)." Lewis (1994) writes that, "Because large classes provide a great deal of anonymity, students frequently feel that they can talk to their neighbors, come or leave when they feel like it, and so forth, without suffering any kind of consequences."

Lewis suggests that instructors make a statement about their expectations of the students and their responsibilities to themselves and to their fellow classmates. Sometimes, students feel that the back of a large lecture theatre is a place to sit and chat with friends, or even a convenient place to have lunch when they are not even taking the course. Some lecture halls I have visited were so noisy that it was almost impossible to hear the instructor.

Much of the problem of uninvolved students is the teaching method employed in the circumstances. While this book does describe a number of different instructional strategies a number of them are not the easiest to employ in a large class situation. Almost inevitably, then, the lecture is the instructional method most usually employed with large classes.

 But if one is lecturing a large class, how does one make students interested, and hold their interest? Enthusiasm for your teaching and for your subject is the key.

As Weaver and Cottrell (1987) note, "If there is one instructor characteristic related to learning it is enthusiasm....The simplest person, fired with enthusiasm, is more persuasive than the most eloquent person without it."

If you are going to hold students' attention, it is important to vary the presentation. Interspersing a lecture with audiovisual materials, demonstrations, and short student activities all help to keep students' attention.

A two-minute pause every 12-15 minutes or so, is a good way of restoring student energy, allowing the students a break from writing, and gives them an opportunity of reviewing their notes and discussing them with their classmates (See Figures 5.1 and 5.2). Interspersing the lecture with a variety of student-based activities is important in any teaching situation, but is especially important in large classes.

You should have a number of other activities ready to use at different times of the semester, but if you are new to teaching you should develop a few to try out, and each semester add new ones so that you eventually have quite a few to use as circumstances permit.

The easiest ones to try are these three:

- short demonstrations (especially if you have a student or two to assist you)

- setting problems for students to solve individually or in groups

- small group discussions to answer questions you pose

Remember that if you don't have such an activity to use in a particular lecture period, you can always employ the two-minute pause, making the purpose of the pause clear to the students.

In a large class, remember that the class is probably very heterogeneous and has a wide variety of learning styles. Try to address all the learning styles during the course of a lecture. Thus, in addition to talking—which addresses the aural learning style— make use of visuals such as overheads, PowerPoint slides, models etc. to address the needs of visual learners. Kinesthetic learners are more difficult to accommodate in a large class situation, since they need to handle items and move around. Strategies that involve them in demonstrations are important. Of course laboratory sessions are also well adapted for kinesthetic students' learning styles.

Communications

Since students in large classes are less likely to want to make comments or ask questions in front of their peers, the instructor may have to elicit communication with his/her students in a variety of ways.

One way is to ask students to form small groups to discuss a question posed to the class and then to ask groups to give an answer. While it is not feasible to ask every group for an answer, you will receive a fair number of answers as students, in the group format, may be more willing to speak in the larger classes. This question/answer strategy can be used throughout the semester, and as it becomes a familiar activity more groups will be prepared to offer answers. You can get almost instantaneous feedback from students with electronic "clickers," or non-technological versions such as cardboard cubes with different responses on each side, or even colored cards (with different colors on the two sides).

Another interesting idea from Lewis (1994) is the use of question boxes placed near the door(s) in which students can place their written questions or comments, and which the instructor can answer in the next class. Of course there are a variety of technology-based options for students to ask questions, make comments and the like including e-mail, web forums, blogs, Twitter etc....

Other simple feedback options include the one-minute paper and the class questionnaire. Lewis (1994) suggests the one-minute paper given at the end of class asks the students to answer two short questions:

1. "What was the most important idea you learned during to-day's class?"

2. "What questions do you still have about the material discussed today?"

Another option, the brief questionnaire, takes students about five minutes to complete.

Student response groups—a small group of students with whom the instructor meets every two weeks—is another tool that may be used. Other class members are encouraged to pass on their comments to the response group. You can even have informal open coffee sessions. Invite students to have coffee, and discuss the course with you.

Tests and Assignments

Clearly, testing and marking written assignments for large classes can be a challenge. Here are a number of tips that can help make the task a bit less daunting:

1. Use a number of tests/exams but don't count all of them in calculating a student's final mark. Under this scheme, students can drop a low score, or can miss a test without you having to give *any* make-up exams.

2. Have a protocol/policy in place to deal with students asking for re-reads of papers, and stick to it.

3. Written assignments do not have to be onerously long. Assign 1000-word writing projects and/or micro-themes.

4. Use an assignment hand-out. Not only does it make marking much easier, but it also reduces significantly the numbers of students asking for re-marks since they can see from the attachment where their strong and weak points are.

5. If you have the use of TA's (teaching assistants) do not use them for grading subjective responses on tests and assignments – it will result in too much variability in grading standards. Use them to mark the more content-style questions. You should be the one to grade written assignments and essay questions.

Teaching Assistants

You may be lucky enough to be assigned TA's to help in large classes. So how best to make use of TA's? I primarily use TA's to help in proctoring exams and grading those exams, but I have also used them, depending on their background and experience, to assist in teaching (if I am away), holding office hours (in addition to mine), and even running tutorials and remedial or revision classes. It is always important to meet with them as a group first to explain how you intend to make use of them, and the way you would like them to work with you and the class.

For grading tests, I give each of them a copy of the answer sheet in advance, and ask them to mark a few papers the first evening after a test, and ask each of them to call me at home, or contact me by e-mail, if they have any concerns. Any questions are answered and problems solved before too many of the tests are completely graded. I may even gather them together the next day so that we can all go through the graded exams, and make any necessary adjustments.

Remember that teaching large classes can be fun and exhilarating.

I find teaching very small classes much more challenging than teaching larger ones. Heppner, in *Teaching the Large College Class* (2007), writes, "Teaching large classes well is the most difficult and challenging task in academia and offers the fewest tangible rewards. Knowing, however, that you have a real, positive, and inspiring effect on hundreds or thousands of young people will more than compensate for the liabilities. Do it right and you will have former students all over the world who will be grateful to you for the wisdom you gave them."

Figure 9.1—Cartoon

"We've raised the student cap."

Top Ten Tips for Teaching Large Classes and Lectures

1. Ensure that course materials and resources are accessible to all by following the Universal Design for Learning model.

2. Be active in the classroom/auditorium. Move around the class and invite participation. This will help create an encouraging environment so that neither you nor your students will feel intimidated by the numbers.

3. Personalize your class; get to know as many names as possible. Extend your availability—show up to class early and be sure to keep regular office hours.

4. Integrate active learning strategies that are focused on specific outcomes. Consider using "clickers" for attendance, quizzes, and to generate discussions.

5. Encourage participation by building things into the lesson that are generally not an experience one could get in other ways—debates, guest speakers, films, etc.

6. Create working teams or small groups of students for discussion and in-class work.

7. Put a "help" box in the classroom so that more reticent students can ask course or homework questions anonymously; budget time for your response at the beginning or end of the next class meeting.

8. Provide feedback to students often; short quizzes, outlines, bibliographies, summaries, etc.

9. Utilize teaching assistants effectively, both for administrative duties, such as attendance, and instructional duties, such as facilitating group work.

10. Creative student projects, whether for extra credit or as part of the requirements, can help personalize the course experience, making students feel more invested.

From: The Center for Teaching and Faculty Development, San Francisco State University (http://ctfd.sfsu.edu/)

CHAPTER 10
TEACHING ONLINE

Getting Started

So, your teaching schedule calls for you to teach a distance education course. It doesn't matter if this is your first such venture, or you have taught at a distance before—it should be approached as if it were your first ever. Recall that when you decided to enter the teaching profession, you looked to the human interaction with students as a major factor in your decision. You were to be the conductor, and every class a symphony with lots of direction and emotion involved in the production (class). Now you are about to enter a new arena. As such, you must view yourself as an engineer on a train. The train has many cars—each is loaded with different course delivery technologies which you will need to call upon to reach your destination (objectives). The goods you must deliver, the students, are in the last car. Sometimes, you can't even see them.

This chapter will provide you the skills necessary to complete your journey—through the use of technology. However, as with teaching face-to-face, preparation is necessary. In fact, perhaps it's even slightly more important. In a classroom, it is easy to recover from a mishap or an error; in a distance learning situation, it is much more difficult. There are two major factors that you must keep in mind while preparing for your distance education courses: you must have complete command of the technology, and you must not lose sight of the fact that the human touch alluded to earlier is not de-emphasized, but is, in fact, emphasized as much as possible.

Master the technology, but do not get so wrapped up in it that individual students are neglected! The same basic premises apply to a distance education course—keep the lines of communication open, and always be well prepared.

Online Lingo 101

Is your ISP up and your URL down? Not sure if you need to know the difference between HTTP and HTML?

On page 138 there is a glossary of the most common technical terms associated with distance education and the Internet. As a part-time faculty member assigned to teach in an online program, do you need to know all of the terms before you begin your classes? No. You will, however, come across many of these terms while teaching courses online.

Your Assignment: Skim the glossary. Stop and read the definitions of a few of the terms with which you may be familiar. Read a few of the terms you've never heard before.

Extra Credit: Incorporate the necessary terms, where appropriate, into your course description and syllabus. Make sure your students understand and use them correctly.

Technological Preparation

When it comes to computers, count on Murphy's Law: if something can go wrong, it will. So to avoid crises ranging from delayed access to destroyed data, plan ahead. Having confidence in your tools will increase your own confidence in teaching. Here are a few tips. Share them with your students, as well:

Virus protection: Virus protection software is a necessity, especially if you plan to download any attachments from students onto your home computer. Virus protection is available online for an annual subscription fee (which may be tax deductible); the two leading providers are McAfee (http://www.mcafee.com/us/) and Norton (http://www.symantec.com).

Adware and spyware detection software: Most current computer problems are caused by adware (free software) and spyware (software surreptitiously installed on your computer to track your virtual activity). Among the free tools available to help rid your computer of these electronic parasites are Ad-Aware (http://www. lavasoftusa.com/) and Spybot (http://www.safer-networking.org/ en/spybotsd/), which scan your computer and identify intrusive software that is present.

Surge protection: Be sure you have a good surge suppressor that will protect your computer during power surges and lightning strikes. For adequate protection, choose a surge suppressor with a "UL 1449" rating of at least 330V and a joule rating of at least 800V.

Computer back-ups: Be sure to back up all critical information onto CD's or other storage devices such as a USB drive (which is also great for portably storing student papers if you work at different computers). If you don't have a second computer, scout out computers you can use if yours fails: at your workplace, at a friend's or relative's house, at the local college or public library, or at a local Internet cafe.

ISP back-ups: You also need to be prepared for your Internet service to fail. It's good to have a second ISP in place for that eventuality. The best option is to sign up for free limited Internet service (usually 10 free hours per month) from at least one provider such as NetZero (http://www.netzero.com) or Juno (http://www.juno.com). This web page offers an extensive database of free ISPs by country: http://www.free-internet.name/country/United-States/

Design and Content Preparation

Inexperienced online teachers are surprised by the amount of time involved not only in creating a course, but also in facilitating it. A 1999-2000 study conducted by Belinda Davis Lazarus, a faculty member in education at the University of Michigan-Dearborn, gives some insight into the time commitment required. Lazarus's longitudinal case study found that an experienced instructor of three online education courses spent 3.5 to 7.0 hours per week on each course. The time was spent responding to student e-mails, participating in discussions, and grading.

A significant difference in teaching online is that there is much more advanced preparation necessary. Instructors accustomed to deciding what to do in each class the night before will find the transition particularly overwhelming, for an effective and well-organized online classroom is one where all material is posted from the start. Here are some tips to help ease the transition to the online classroom:

1. Visit sample online classrooms to get a sense of what works and what doesn't, and to better recognize your own online teaching style. Many colleges offer sample course sites for prospective students to explore, but they're also great resources for the adjunct new to online learning. Here are a few:

- The Connecticut Distance Learning Consortium sample courses using three course management systems (WebCT, Blackboard, and WebMentor): http://www.ctdlc.org/Sample/guest.html

- University of Wisconsin: http://learn.wisconsin.edu/course.asp

- University of Wisconsin Stevens Points: http://www.uwsp.edu/natres/nres600/main.htm

- Weber State University: http://departments.weber.edu/ce/distancelearning/demo.aspx

2. Start simply. You don't have to incorporate all the technological bells and whistles as you begin; trying to do so will only overwhelm you. For example, if you want to incorporate live chat, but aren't sure about how it will work, you can make such interaction an option in your first course rather than a requirement. Once you understand the technology, you'll feel better able to construct a more intricate system of group activities and discussions. "The Online Course Design Maturity Model" (Neuhauser, 2004) identifies five levels of sophistication and quality across five areas: components and appearance, individualized and personal approach, use of technology, socialization and interactivity, and assessment. The levels of assessment, for example, would progress from no online assignments, to assignments received through e-mail, to test pools, to peer reviews, to more multi-faceted assignments. For more information visit the Summer 2003 issue of *Journal of Interactive and Online Learning* here: http://www.ncolr.org/jiol/issues

3. Set tight and frequent deadlines. Consider segmenting each assignment so that one part of it is due each day. This helps prevent students from procrastinating. Make deadlines absolute, but build in crisis cushions; for example, you might allow one assignment to be turned in two days late with no penalty, but then penalize students five points for each day other assignments are late no matter what the reason.

Tips For Working Efficiently

To save time, set limits on the time spent on the computer; encourage more student-to-student interaction, and make better use of time-saving technology. Here are some specific suggestions:

- Block out times during which you will be available to students.

- Don't respond to every student on the discussion board. Allow students to moderate discussions; they can answer each other's publicly posted questions so that the instructor isn't always expected to do so. In fact, if you respond too quickly, you can inhibit student responses.

- Have students collaborate on group projects. This results in interactions that don't involve the instructor, and in fewer papers to grade.

- Save and reuse your discussion board postings from one semester to the next.

- Create a FAQ (Frequently Asked Questions) page so that you're not constantly answering the same questions.

- Use computer-graded quizzes.

- Assemble a body of Internet links related to your course, and build on it each semester through your own searches, as well as by assigning students to compile and annotate a list of course-related Web sites.

- Have assignments due at mid-week rather than at the end of the week, especially if you want to stay away from the computer during the weekend.

- Make sure students have passed an orientation quiz or completed an online scavenger hunt at the start of the semester so that they know how to navigate the course; this will reduce the number of questions later.

- Require that students send work as .txt (text) files if formatting is not an issue, and as .rtf (rich text format) files when formatting is important. This will minimize your download time, and problems related to software conflicts.

- Bookmark the course Web site, and write down the password information and tech help phone number; keep both near your computer and in your wallet for when you're working remotely on a computer where this information has not been saved.

Accessibility

Since 1998, when Congress amended the Rehabilitation Act, federal agencies have been required under Section 508 of the law to make electronic and information technology accessible to those with disabilities. Coupled with the older and more inclusive Americans with Disabilities Act, there is a greater emphasis on creating online courses that can be used by everyone.

One of the first things the part-time faculty member can do to make her/his course more accessible is to post in different formats. For example, an assignment may be posted as a Web page and also in PDF format. A lecture may be posted in text and in

PowerPoint outline form, but once you've been teaching online for awhile, you'll probably want to go further. For instance, you might create HTML tags for illustrations to help the blind or avoid certain colors for those with color blindness. Look at your entire site and its ease of use for those with various disabilities. Here are some free tools that can help:

- A list of the requirements for Section 508: http://www. access-board.gov/sec508/guide/1194.22.htm

- Web Accessibility Initiative, a good overview: http://www.w3.org/WAI/Resources/

- Advice on how to design more usable Web sites: http://trace.wisc.edu/world/web/

- Tips for designing accessible Web sites, divided by disability and tool: http://diveintoaccessibility.org/

- CynthiaSays! is a Web content accessibility validation solution, designed to identify errors in design related to Section 508 standards and the Web Content Accessibility Guidelines. This service is a free accessibility validation tester: http://www.cynthiasays.com/

- Accessibility checklist from Penn State University offers guidelines for designing or modifying Web pages for accessibility: http://webstandards.psu.edu/accessibility

- Adobe offers information and tools to make PDF files accessible: http://www.adobe.com/accessibility/tutorials.html

- Microsoft offers tutorials for using accessibility features in Windows, Word, Outlook, and Internet Explorer: http://www.microsoft.com/enable/training/default.aspx

- Vischeck allows you to see what Web sites look like for those who are color blind: http://www.vischeck.com/vischeck/

Community Building

In teaching a distance education course you are, in a sense, building your own little community. You are not just the facilitator; you are the mayor. Your #1 goal is to keep the citizens from moving out.

Attrition rates for most distance education programs have been higher than for traditional college courses, with dropout rates as high as 80 percent at some colleges, though this trend is changing as programs mature. Many of the reasons—such as students' inexperience with technology, or insufficient student support services—are beyond a part-timer's control. However, you can have a tremendous impact on student retention simply by the way you communicate. The form, frequency, promptness, and tone of written and oral interaction with students are very important.

The trick is to create a sense of classroom community. If students feel connected, if they believe that you have a personal interest in them, they will be less likely to drop out. Research by Angie Parker, who teaches at Yavapai College, shows that those students with a higher "internal locus of control," or level of self-motivation, were more likely to complete a course. For students taking distance education courses, such an internal control was even more important, because these students must function more independently. This self-motivation is a learned trait, but it develops more readily through positive reinforcement; if students in online classes feel that they're alone as they struggle with the technology as well as the course material, they are in greater danger of dropping out. In distance education, Parker concludes, "Instructional intervention can be a powerful tool for accelerating motivational change."

The dramatic increase in the number of online courses at colleges and universities—and the problem of hanging on to students unprepared for this new way of learning—are leading to some research efforts aimed at systematically examining both issues. "Quality on the Line: Benchmarks for Success in Internet-Based Distance Education" (2004), a study by the Institute for Higher

Education Policy, recommends that contact between faculty and students be "facilitated through a variety of ways, including voice-mail and/or e-mail" and that "Feedback to student assignments and questions is constructive and provided in a timely manner." Communication, the study concludes, is key. In discussing community online, Gary Wheeler (Wheeler, 2002) quotes a study by Palloff and Pratt that defines the basic steps for establishing a virtual community. The steps are:

- Clearly define the purpose of the group

- Create a distinctive gathering place for the group

- Promote effective leadership within the group

- Define norms and a clear code of conduct

- Allow for a range of member roles

- Allow for and facilitate subgroups

- Allow members to resolve their own disputes.

It appears that allowing students to resolve their own conflicts results in improved communication within the group. Since face-to-face interchange is not possible, online discussions in which students present conflicting viewpoints seem to introduce a degree of emotion into the learning process. However, you must be careful to monitor the conflict so that it does not deteriorate into personal issues and discourage dialogue.

One way to do this to set a positive tone from the start. Instructors can do this by being personal, polite, open and responsive in communications you have with individual students, and with the class as a whole. When responding to students' questions and comments on the discussion board and in e-mail, always use their names, and consider signing messages with your first name, which seems friendlier. Make frequent use of terms like "please" and "thanks." All of this takes extra time, but it's worth it.

While it's a good idea to keep most communication on the discussion board so that you don't end up repeatedly answering the same question, e-mail can be a great tool for personal encouragement and for friendly reminders about assignments that are upcoming or overdue. To keep students on task, send weekly e-mails to those who did not post on the discussion board to let them know their contributions were missed. Another way to encourage communication is to make yourself available at times and in a manner that is most helpful for students. This doesn't mean that, as an adjunct, you need to chain yourself to your computer 24/7, but it might mean that you hold an online office hour one evening a week, perhaps the night before an assignment is due. Make it easy for students to contact you instantly, either in a chat room through the courseware or via Instant Messaging.

Practical Tips for Good Communication in Online Courses:

Call students on the phone. This is a simple and overlooked "low-tech" tool that can be very effective early in the term, especially for students who haven't gotten started yet. It's a way to show you're interested and to answer questions — usually technical — that may have them stymied.

Build a learning community. Have students post written introductions (and photographs if possible) on the discussion board — and post one yourself. Encourage students to interact with discussions about course material, either through a space on your site or in temporary chat rooms. Create an area online for socializing.

Give frequent and encouraging feedback. You might adapt the practices of a biology instructor at Piedmont Technical College in Greenwood, South Carolina, who holds online office hours, responds to e-mail within 24 hours, gives a range of dates for an exam to be completed, and responds to students individually with their grades and where they stand in the course.

Maximize the use of the discussion board to encourage group interaction. Minimize the use of e-mail for communication, and keep communication on the discussion board as much as possible.

Check in daily to answer questions and redirect discussions if they get off track. Students need to sense your presence though you don't want to intrude. Some instructors post on discussion boards a few times during the week while others write a weekly posting which comments directly on what students have had to say during the week. Even if a problem seems to be developing, hold back, for often the group will resolve its own conflicts and be stronger for it. But if discussions veer wildly off track, post a follow-up question to help recapture the focus.

Be encouraging, understanding, and flexible. Congratulate students on a good grade. Ask what happened when a grade was low. Allow them some time flexibility in completing assignments, if possible. Share a little of yourself. Reach out to students who are struggling. A simple note to a student asking, "Is everything OK? I haven't heard from you in a while," can give a student under great pressure the reassurance that someone cares.

Make class fun. Bramucci (2001) offers many ideas for injecting an impish spirit and for giving students reasons to check into the class more often. For example, he suggests a weekly "Guess who?" feature based on unusual facts gathered by the teacher about each student. "Hide" actual test questions on the site in a sort of "Where's Waldo?" activity. Post teasers about interesting information to be covered in an upcoming lesson. Post holiday greetings. Invite students to submit nominations for a joke of the week.

Use an Icebreaker. Maybe more so than with a class taught face-to-face, an icebreaker can be an asset for distance education classes. It commences communication immediately, gives the students a chance to participate and use the technology, and gives the instructor an opportunity to observe student writing styles.

Diving Into the Wreck: Revisiting Online Classrooms After the Semester Ends

by Rich Russell, "Teaching in Pajamas" blog, AdjunctNation.com, January 18, 2011.

It is that time, just before the new semester begins, when the online professor must again go diving into the wreck.

Well— but it was not a wreck, exactly; wreck has such a negative connotation. Something beautiful there-existed (still exists) that, after grades were entered, was allowed to drown — to quietly expire: the students denied access to the online course as the clock struck midnight at the end of the Fall term.

When a traditional class is over, it is over (done): the students hand in their final exam or final papers, exit stage-right, and that is all she wrote, so to speak. Sometimes there are frantic queries sent — desperate pleas ("oh, please, professor…!") for a clemency of additional points added. But mostly, as I admit to them on the final class when I thank them for their enthusiasm and commitment, "Some of us may never see one another again: and that is the reality of life." (I know, a bit existential; how fitting that our last unit in Introduction to Literature this term was titled "The Presence of Death.") There is always that moment on the final class when one wonders (or at least I do), after a student has turned in the final, will she say anything? — will he just leave, not look back, in a "now on to the next thing" sort of way? Most of my students like to hang around after the last class, not wishing for it all to end so soon, like drowsy revelers lingering after a splendid party. Still, I'm most fascinated by the steely resolve of those who just go and who do not look back for fear of turning into sodium chloride (so bad for the cholesterol, after all).

Online, though, there isn't really a last class. At about this time, a week before the new semester starts, I find myself returning to those cities that were constructed over the fifteen weeks: the classrooms that have been neglected over winter break, buried in the ash. This is a return to the world of ghosts: all of those past discussions and assignments, all perfectly preserved, as if the students were still talking to one another and to me. Here one finds the truthy urn of Keats: every "LOL" and each passing disagreement frozen in a noisy yet silent form. I must admit, I find it a bit unsettling to have to revisit this place, now that the authors have all abandoned the ship, leaving me to clean up, to salvage all that worked and leave behind anything that did not.

The professor alone must return to the wreck, to turn back on the lights and have a look around before hitting the reset button.

Glossary of Online Terminology

Analog: A signal that is received in the same form in which it is transmitted, while the amplitude and frequency may vary.

Amplitude: The amount of variety in a signal. Commonly thought of as the height of a wave.

American Standard Code for Information Interexchange (ASCII): A computer language used to convert letters, numbers, and control codes into a digital code understood by most computers.

Asynchronous: Communication in which interaction between parties does not take place simultaneously.

Asynchronous Transmission Mode (ATM): A method of sending data in irregular time intervals using a code such as ASCII. ATM allows most modern computers to communicate with one another easily.

Audio Bridge: A device used in audioconferencing that connects multiple telephone lines.

Audioconferencing: Voice only connection of more than two sites using standard telephone lines.

Backbone: A primary communication path connecting multiple users.

Band: A range of frequencies between defined upper and lower limits.

Bandwidth: Information carrying capacity of a communication channel.

Binary: A computer language developed with only two letters in its alphabet.

Bit: Abbreviation for a single binary digit.

Byte: A single computer word, generally eight bits.

Browser: Software that allows you to find and see information on the Internet.

Central Processing Unit (CPU): The component of a computer in which data processing takes place.

Channel: The smallest subdivision of a circuit, usually with a path in only one direction.

Codec (COder/DECoder): Device used to convert analog signals to digital signals for transmission and reconvert signals upon reception at the remote site while allowing for the signal to be compressed for less expensive transmission.

Compressed Video: When video signals are downsized to allow travel along a smaller carrier.

Compression: Reducing the amount of visual information sent in a signal by only transmitting changes in action.

Computer Assisted Instruction (CAI): Teaching process in which a computer is utilized to enhance the learning environment by assisting students in gaining mastery over a specific skill.

Cyberspace: The nebulous "place" where humans interact over computer networks. Coined by William Gibson in *Neuromancer*.

Desktop Videoconferencing: Videoconferencing on a personal computer.

Dial-Up Teleconference: Using public telephone lines for communications links among various locations.

Digital: An electrical signal that varies in discrete steps in voltage, frequency, amplitude, locations, etc.... Digital signals can be transmitted faster and more accurately than analog signals.

Digital Video Interactive (DVI): A format for recording digital video onto compact disc allowing for compression and full motion video.

Distance Education: The process of providing instruction when students and instructors are separated by physical distance and technology, often in tandem with face-to-face communication, is used to bridge the gap.

Distance Learning: The desired outcome of distance education.

Download: Using the network to transfer files from one computer to another.

Echo Cancellation: The process of eliminating the acoustic echo in a videoconferencing room.

Electronic Mail (E-mail): Sending messages from one computer user to another.

Facsimile (FAX): System used to transmit textual or graphical images over standard telephone lines.

Fiber Optic Cable: Glass fiber that is used for laser transmission of video, audio, and/or data.

File Transfer Protocol (FTP): A protocol that allows you to move files from a distant computer to a local computer using a network like the Internet.

Frequency: The space between waves in a signal. The amount of time between waves passing a stationary point.

Frequently Asked Questions (FAQ): A collection of information on the basics of any given subject, often used on the WWW.

Full Motion Video: Signal which allows transmission of complctc action taking place at the origination site.

Fully Interactive Video: (Two way interactive video) Two sites interact with audio and video as if they were co-located.

Home Page: A document with an address (URL) on the World Wide Web maintained by a person or organization which contains pointers to other pieces of information.

Host: A network computer that can receive information from other computers.

Hyper Text Markup Language (HTML): The code used to create a home page and is used to access documents over the WWW.

Hypertext Transfer Protocol (HTTP): The protocol used to signify an Internet site is a WWW site, i.e. HTTP is a WWW address.

Hypertext: A document which has been marked up to allow a user to select words or pictures within the document, click on them, and connect to further information.

Instructional Television Fixed Service (ITFS): Microwave-based, high-frequency television used in educational program delivery.

Integrated Services Digital Network (ISDN): A telecommunications standard allowing communications channels to carry voice, video, and data simultaneously.

Interactive Media: Frequency assignment that allows for a two-way interaction or exchange of information.

Internet Service Provider (ISP): An organization that provides access to the Internet. Connection to the user is provided via dial-up, ISDN, cable, DSL, T1/T3 lines or fiber.

Listserv: An e-mail program that allows multiple computer users to connect onto a single system, creating an online discussion.

Local Area Network (LAN): Two or more local computers that are physically connected.

Modem: A piece of equipment to allow computers to interact with each other via telephone lines by converting digital signals to analog for transmission along analog lines.

Mosaic: An example of browser software that allows WWW use.

Multimedia: Any document which uses multiple forms of communication, such as text, audio, and/or video.

Multi-Point Control Unit (MCU): Computerized switching system which allows point-to-multipoint videoconferencing.

Netscape: An example of browser software that allows you to design a home page and to browse links on the WWW.

Network: A series of points connected by communication channels in different locations.

Online: Active and prepared for operation. Also suggests access to a computer network.

Origination Site: The location from which a teleconference originates.

Point of Presence (POP): Point of connection between an interexchange carrier and a local carrier to pass communications into the network.

Point-to-Point: Transmission between two locations.

Point-to-Multipoint: Transmission among multiple locations using a bridge.

PPP: A software package which allows a user to have a direct connection to the Internet over a telephone line.

Protocol: A formal set of standards, rules, or formats for exchanging data that assures uniformity between computers and applications.

Satellite TV: Video and audio signals that are relayed via a communication device that orbits around the earth.

Serial Line Internet Protocol (SLIP): Allows a user to connect to the Internet directly over a high speed modem.

Server: A computer with a special service function on a network, generally receiving and connecting incoming information traffic.

Slow Scan Converter: Transmitter/receiver of still video over narrow band channels. In real time, camera subjects must remain still for highest resolution.

Synchronous: Communication in which interaction among participants is simultaneous.

T-1 (DS-1): High speed digital data channel that is a high volume carrier of voice and/or data. Often used for compressed video teleconferencing. T-1 has 24 voice channels.

T-3 (DS-3): A digital channel which communicates at a significantly faster rate than T-1.

Telecommunication: The science of information transport using wire, radio, optical, or electromagnetic channels to transmit and receive signals for voice or data communications using electrical means.

Teleconferencing: Two way electronic communication among two or more groups in separate locations via audio, video, and/or computer systems.

Transmission Control Protocol (TCP): A protocol which makes sure that packets of data are shipped and received in the intended order.

Transponder: Satellite transmitter and receiver that receives and amplifies a signal prior to re-transmission to an earth station.

Video Teleconferencing: A teleconference including two way video.

Uniform Resource Locator (URL): The address of a homepage on the WWW.

Uplink: The communication link from the transmitting earth station to the satellite.

World Wide Web (WWW): A graphical hypertext-based Internet tool that provides access to homepages created by individuals, businesses, and other organizations.

References

Angelo, T.A. 1991. "Learning in the classroom (Phase I)." A report from the Lawrence Hall of Science, University of California at Berkeley, California.

Angelo T. & Cross K. 1993. *Classroom Assessment Techniques: A Handbook for College Teachers* (2nd ed.). San Francisco: Jossey-Bass.

Atkinson, M., Wilson, T., and Kidd, J. 2008. "Virtual education: teaching and learning in Second Life." *Teaching and Learning in Higher Education*, 50:1.

Bianco-Mathis, V. et al. 1996. *The Adjunct Faculty Handbook*. Thousand Oaks, CA: Sage Publications, Inc.

Bligh, D.A. 1971. *What's the Use of Lectures?* Exeter, Devon: D.A., and B. Bligh.

Bligh, D. A. 2000. *What's the Use of Lectures?* San Francisco: Jossey-Bass.

Bloom, B. et. al. 1956. *Taxonomy of Educational Objectives*. New York: David McKay.

Bramucci, R. 2001. "Ideas for distance learning." Retrieved September 11, 2004 from the World Wide Web: <http://fdc.fullerton.edu/learning/STG2001_IDEAS.htm>.

Brownstein, E., and Klein, R. 2006. "Blogs — applications in science education." *Journal of College Science Teaching*, XXXV, 6:18-22.

Burnstad, H. 2000. "Developing the environment for learning." In Greive D, (ed.). *Handbook II-Advanced Teaching Strategies for Adjunct and Part-time Faculty*. Ann Arbor, MI: Part-Time Press.

Cann, A., Badge, J., Johnson, S., and Moseley, A. 2009. "Twittering the students experience." *Association for Learning Technology Online Newsletter*, Issue 17, Monday, 19 October, 2009.

Cooper, J.L., and Robinson, P. 2000. "The argument for making large classes seem small." *New Directions for Teaching and Learning*. 81, 63-76.

de Fondeville, T. 2009. "Ten steps to better student engagement." Edutopia.com <http://www.edutopia.org/project-learning-teaching-strategies.>

Duncan, D. 2005. *Clickers in the Classroom: How to Enhance Science Teaching Using Classroom Response Systems.* San Francisco: Pearson Education/Addison-Wesley/Benjamin Cummings.

Eisner, S. 2004. "Teaching generation Y college students: three initiatives." *Journal of College Teaching and Learning,* 1(9) , 69-84.

Erickson, B.L., and Strommer, D.W. 1991. *Teaching College Freshmen.* San Francisco: Jossey-Bass.

Fletcher, A. 2009. "Defining student engagement: A literature review." SoundOut.org <http://www.soundout.org/student-engagement-AF.pdf.>

Greive, D. (Ed.). 2000. *Handbook II-Advanced Teaching Strategies for Adjunct and Part-time Faculty.* Ann Arbor, MI: Part-Time Press.

Guthrie, R.W., and Carlin, A. 2004. "Waking the dead: using interactive technology to engage passive listeners in the classroom." Proceedings of the Tenth Americas Conference on Information Systems, New York.

Hartley, J., and Davies, I.K. 1978. "Note-taking: a critical review." *Programmed Learning and Educational Technology,* 15, 3, 207-224.

Heppner, F. 2009. *Teaching the Large College Class: A Guidebook for Instructors with Multitudes.* San Francisco: Jossey-Bass.

Herreid, C.F. 2006. "Clicker" cases: introducing case study teaching into large classrooms." *Journal of College Science Teaching,* XXXVI, 2,43-47.

Johnson, B. 2010, November. Blog entry: "Student engagement—why it matters, parts I, II, III." <http://www.AdjunctNation.com>

Jones, R. 2008. "Strengthening student engagement." International Center for Leadership in Education. <http://www.leadered.com/pdf/Strengthen%20Student%20Engagement%20white%20paper.pdf.>

Knowles, M. 1990. *The Adult Learner-A Neglected Species.* Houston, TX: Gulf Publishing.

Lay, Robert. 2000. "Demographic change and emerging talent pools." *Company Magazine.* 42, 53-60.

Lazarus, B. D. "Teaching courses online: How much time does it take?" *Journal of Asynchronous Learning Networks,*7(3). Retrieved November 9, 2004 from the World Wide Web: <http://www.sloan-c.org/publications/jaln/v7n3/v7n3_lazarus.asp>.

Lewis, K.G. 1994. "Teaching large classes (How to do it well and remain sane)." In Prichard, K.W., and Sawyer, R.M. (eds.). *Handbook of College Teaching: Theory and Application,* p. 319-343. London: Greenwood Press.

Lloyd, D.H. 1968. "A concept of improvement of learning response in the taught lesson." *Visual Education,* October, 23-25.

Mager, R. 1962. *Preparing Instructional Objectives.* Belmont, CA: Fearon Publishers.

McCarthy, B. 1987. *The 4-MAT System.* Barrington, IL: Excel, Inc.

McKeachie, W. et. al. 1994. *Teaching Tips, Srategies, Research and Theory for College and University Teachers.* Lexington, MA: D. C. Heath and Co.

McLeish, J. 1968. *The Lecture Method. Cambridge Monographs on Teaching Methods.* Cambridge, U.K.: Cambridge Institute of Education.

NEA, 1975. <www.new.org/aboutnea/code.html.>

Neuhauser, C. "A maturity model: Does it provide a path for online course design?" *Journal of Interactive Online Learning,* 3(1). Retrieved August 30, 2004 from the World Wide Web: <http://www.ncolr.org/jiol/issues/>.

New England Literacy Resource Center, 2009. "Drivers of persistence." <http://www.nelrc.org/persist/drivers_belonging.html>

Palloff, R. M., & Pratt, K. 2003. *The Virtual Student: A Profile and Guide to Working with Online Learners.* San Francisco: Jossey-Bass.

Palmer, C. 2009. "Building student engagement: classroom atmosphere." FacultyFocus.com <http://www.facultyfocus.com/articles/effective-classroom-management/building-student-enga.>

Parker, A. "Identifying predictors of academic persistence in distance education." *USDLA Journal,*17(1). Retrieved November 9, 2004 from the World Wide Web: <http://www.usdla.org/html/journal/JAN03_Issue/article06.html>.

"Quality on the line: Benchmarks for success in Internet-based distance education." 2004. The Institute for Higher Education Policy. Retrieved August 30, 2004 from the World Wide Web: <http://www.ihep.com/Pubs/PDF/Quality.pdf>.

Ruhl, K.L., Hughes, C.A., and Schloss, P.J. 2007. "Using the Pause Procedure to enhance lecture recall." *Teacher Education and Special Education*, 10(1),14-18.

Russell, R. 2011, January. Blog entry: "Diving Into the Wreck: Revisiting Online Classrooms After the Semester Ends" <http://www.AdjunctNation.com>

Salomon, J. 1994. "The diverse classroom." In Frye, B. (ed). *Teaching in College-A Resource for College Teachers*. Elyria OH: Info-Tec.

Sego, A. 1994. *Cooperative Learning-A Classroom Guide*. Elyria, OH: Info-Tec.

Stephan, K., 2000. "The syllabus and the lesson plan." In Greive, D. (ed). *Handbook II-Advanced Teaching Strategies for Adjunct and Part-time Faculty*. Ann Arbor, MI: Part-Time Press.

Weaver, R.L., and Cotrell, H.W. 1987. "Lecturing: essential communication strategies." In Weimer, M.G. (Ed.). *Teaching Large Classes Well. New Directions for Teaching and Learning*, no. 32, 57-69. San Francisco: Jossey-Bass.

Weimer, M. 1990. *Improving College Teaching*. San Francisco: Jossey-Bass.

Wheeler, Gary S. 2003. *Teaching and Learning in College* (4th ed.). Ann Arbor, MI: Part-Time Press.

Wulff, D. H., Nyquist, J. D., & Abbott, R. D. 1987. "Students' perceptions of large classes." In K. E. Eble (Series Ed.) & M. G. Weimer (Vol. Ed.), *New Directions for Teaching and Learning*: Vol. 32. *Teaching Large Classes Well*. San Francisco: Jossey-Bass.

Yazedjian, A., and Kolkhorst, B.B. 2007. "Implementing small-group activities in large classes." *College Teaching*, 55(4), 164-169.

Index

byte 138

Handbook II: Advanced Strategies for Adjunct and Part-time Faculty by Donald Greive

Handbook II: Advanced Teaching Strategies carries on the tradition of practical and readable instructional guides that began with *A Handbook for Adjunct & Part-time Faculty* (now in its 7th edition!)

Intended for adjuncts who have already mastered the basics and for the managers of adjunct faculty, *Handbook II: Advanced Teaching Strategies* offers in-depth coverage of some of the topics you just read about like andragogy, collaborative learning, syllabus construction, and testing. But this manual also goes beyond these topics to discuss specific teaching techniques for critical thinking, problem solving, large class instruction and distance learning assignments.

Handbook II: Advanced Teaching Strategies gives you expert and current strategies to take your teaching to the next level. Available in paperback for $19.00 each. Also available as a set with *A Handbook for Adjunct & Part-Time Faculty*, $35.00/set.

Going the Distance: A Handbook for Adjunct & Part-Time Faculty Who Teach Online, Revised 1st Edition by Evelyn Beck and Donald Greive, Ed.D.

Whether you're just thinking about teaching online, a first-time online course facilitator, or you are an experienced distance educator, *Going the Distance: A Handbook for Part-Time & Adjunct Faculty Who Teach Online* will help you sharpen your online teaching skills, develop and deliver more richly-structured distance education courses. The revised edition contains updated and expanded sections on blogging, distance education blogs, technology, distance learning conferences, awards & fellowships, and course development. *Going the Distance* is available in paperback for $15.00. Also available as a set with *A Handbook for Adjunct & Part-Time Faculty*, $30.00/set.

FAQ's...

How can I place an orders?

Orders can be placed **by mail** to Part-Time Press, P.O. Box 130117, Ann Arbor, MI 48113-0117, **by phone** at (734)930-6854, **by fax** at (734)665-9001, and **via the Internet** at http://www. Part-TimePress.com.

How much do I pay if I want multiple copies?

Each Part-Time Press book has a quantity discount schedule available. The schedule for *A Handbook for Adjunct & Part-Time Faculty* is:

1-9 copies--$18 each   **10-49 copies**--$15 each
50-99 copies--$13 each   **100 or more copies**--$10 each

How can I pay for orders?

Orders can be placed on **a purchase order** or can be paid by **check** or **credit card** (Visa/Mastercard, Discover or AMEX.)

How will my order be shipped?

Standard shipping to a continental U.S. street address is via **UPS-Ground Service**. Foreign shipments or U.S. post office box addresses go through the **U.S. Postal Service** and express shipments via **UPS-2nd Day**, or **UPS-Next Day**. Shipping and handling charges are based on the dollar amount of the shipment, and a fee schedule is shown on the next page.

What if I'm a reseller like a bookstore or wholesaler?

Resellers get a standard **20 percent discount** off of the single copy retail price, or may choose to receive the multiple copy discount.

Part-Time Press Books: Order Form

Qty	Title	Unit $$	Total
	Handbook for Adjunct/Part-Time Faculty, 7th ed.	**$18.00**	
	Handbook II: Advanced Teaching Strategies	**$19.00**	
	Going the Distance: A Handbook for Part-Time & Adjunct Faculty Who Teach Online, Rev. 1st ed.	**$15.00**	
	Teaching in the Sciences	**$25.00**	
	Getting Down to Business	**$25.00**	
	Teaching Strategies and Techniques, 5th ed.	**$12.00**	
	Managing Adjunct/Part-Time Faculty	**$30.00**	
	Teaching & Learning in College	**$25.00**	
		Subtotal	
		Shipping	
		Total	

Purchaser/Payment Information

☐   *Check (payable to The Part-Time Press)*

☐   *Credit Card #* ———————————————— *Exp.* ————

      CVV# ————————

☐   *Purchase Order #* ————————————————————

Name ————————————————————————————————

Institution ——————————————————————————————

Address ———————————————— *City/ST/Zip* ————————————

Ph:———————————————— *E-mail:* ————————————————

Shipping Schedule:

1-4 books   *$6.00*

5+ books   *8 percent of the purchase price*

Part-Time Press: P.O. Box 130117, Ann Arbor, MI 48113-0117
Ph: 734-930-6854 Fax: 734-665-9001 E-mail: orders@part-timepress.com
Order securely online: http://www.Part-TimePress.com